The Accounting Education Change Commission Grant Experience: A Summary

Edited by

Richard E. Flaherty

American Accounting Association
5717 Bessie Drive
Sarasota, Florida 34233

CONTENTS

FOREWORD

In 1989 the Accounting Education Change Commission (AECC) was formed to improve the academic preparation of accountants, so that entrants to the profession (broadly defined) would possess the skills, knowledge, and values and attitudes required for success in accounting careers. The AECC mission was consistent with the objectives of the American Accounting Association's Bedford Committee report and the Sponsoring Firms' white paper, *"Perspectives on Education: Capabilities for Success in the Accounting Profession."*

Undoubtedly the most visible AECC activity over its seven-year life was the funding of curriculum grants at 13 educational institutions. The purpose of this monograph is to provide a convenient, brief summary of the grant experience at each of these institutions. In general, a similar format is followed in each of the reports to ease your review and comparison of the grant experience at the various schools. They are presented alphabetically by name of the school.

The success of the AECC cannot be measured solely by the results at the grant schools. Only if non-grant schools can learn from these experiences and use the results to enhance the quality of accounting education in their particular institutions will the efforts of the AECC have resulted in widespread improvement in accounting education. Thus, it is our hope that you will read these reports, discuss them, seek additional input from the grant schools as appropriate, and share in the excitement of working to improve accounting education.

Richard E. Flaherty
Executive Director
Accounting Education Change Commission

Chapter 1
ARIZONA STATE UNIVERSITY

Type, Size and Mission of Accounting Program

The mission of the School of Accountancy (SOA) is to prepare students for successful careers in accounting and business, to expand and disseminate knowledge, and to serve the academic, accounting, and business communities. The School will provide an educational environment that facilitates life long learning, including the development of skills and attitudes necessary for professional excellence, continuous improvement, application of information technology, and interaction in a diverse work force. This mission recognizes that graduates need technical accounting knowledge, practical skills, and the ability to function in the local, national and global environments. The SOA is also dedicated to the creation of new knowledge associated with accounting theory, practice and instruction, and to providing service through activities that facilitate professional growth and interaction within the academic, accounting and business communities.

The School offers four degree programs: a bachelor's degree in accountancy, two master's degrees (tax and accounting information management), and a Ph.D. The SOA is also an active participant in the College's three MBA programs (day, evening and executive). In addition, as of January 1996, the Computer Information System (CIS) faculty and related CIS degrees became a part of the School of Accountancy. Effective Fall 1996, undergraduate accountancy majors are required to complete three CIS courses as a part of their degree requirements.

Admission to each degree program is by application. Approximately 250 students are admitted to the undergraduate professional program (junior and senior years) in accountancy each year. The accounting majors in the professional program are almost equally divided on a gender basis. Students admitted to the professional program have an average GPA of 3.50. Being situated in a large metropolitan area, we have a significant number of nontraditional students (part-time and/or older), which enhances the diversity of the learning experience. The Phoenix area has a large number of excellent community colleges; about 50% of our majors are transfer students, the majority from local area community colleges.

The SOA is an active participant in the University's Honors Program which has been ranked in the top ten nationally. Only one other major at ASU (psychology) has more students in the Honors Program than the SOA. The undergraduate and graduate accounting programs have been consistently ranked in the top 20 nationally in the annual Public Accountant Report survey.

Characteristics of Program Before the AECC Grant

The undergraduate program in accounting prior to the AECC grant was very conventional in both approach and what was taught. The lecture method was used as the primary teaching method with minimal use of cases and group activities. The textbook and, to a lesser extent, the CPA examination tended to be the content drivers for most courses. Objective-type examinations dominated most accounting courses. Technical accounting knowledge was emphasized in each accounting course. There was minimal attention given to communication and interpersonal skills in most accounting courses. The solution of textbook type problems was the prevalent and sometimes only type of problem solving required. Cases and unstructured problem solving were at a minimum. Very few significant changes had been made in the undergraduate accounting program for many years. Probably the most significant was the addition of accounting information systems as a required accounting course. There was virtually no use of computer technology to facilitate the learning process.

Despite the now obvious deficiencies in the old program, our graduates were actively recruited and hired by the then Big 8 public accounting firms, local and regional public accounting firms, and a variety of corporations and governmental agencies. In addition, our accounting programs were ranked in the top 20 nationally.

Central Objectives of AECC Grant

Our AECC Curriculum Development Project involved substantial revisions to the accounting portion of the curriculum to better achieve the goals and objectives of the School for the education of our students. In addition to general, business and accounting knowledge, accounting graduates must possess an appropriate level of learning skills, communication skills, analytical skills, and interpersonal skills, as well as entrepreneurial and ethical perspectives.

Central to our curriculum revision was the desire to create an environment in which the student is an active participant in the learning process. Also, a primary goal was to develop in our graduates the ability and motivation for lifelong learning. Key components of our new accounting curriculum include (1) restructuring introductory accounting, (2) providing an information systems foundation for upper-division accounting courses, (3) incorporating a heavy reliance on the case method, (4) use of the cooperative learning/active learning pedagogy, and (5) adopting a laboratory science format for all upper-division accounting courses.

Key Means of Accomplishing the Grant Objectives

In August 1989, the Director of the School of Accountancy appointed a large and diverse faculty committee to review the accounting curriculum in response to the recommendations in the Big 8 White Paper and the Bedford Committee Report. Each of these documents had been discussed at length at the SOA's annual faculty retreats, and there appeared to be a consensus of the faculty that some curriculum changes were in order. During the 1989-90 academic year, the committee developed the basic framework for our new undergraduate curriculum.

Periodically, meetings were held to obtain input from faculty, accounting professionals, employers and students. In addition, input was requested from other academic units in the College of Business. The committee's proposal was discussed in detail at the faculty retreat in September 1990. Shortly after that retreat, the accounting faculty voted overwhelmingly to endorse the proposed changes and to apply to the AECC for funding. The Dean of the College endorsed the proposal and promised to match any amount that was received from the AECC. In addition, the SOA pledged $150,000 to support the project. Commitments were received from several faculty to help develop the new courses and related materials. Much of the course development work was funded through summer grants for both faculty and graduate students. Finally, the endorsement of the upper administration was obtained. The proposal was formalized during October and November. The SOA was informed of the grant award in January 1991.

Major Changes from Pre-Grant Conditions

Introductory Accounting Restructure

The introductory accounting courses are the only accounting courses most business majors will take and represent the first exposure to accounting for many accounting majors. We have restructured these courses into (1) a two-semester, user-oriented sequence that emphasizes the uses and limitations of accounting information (ACC 230 and ACC 240), and (2) a one semester, computer-based instruction course required of all accounting majors that covers the procedural components of accounting needed by accounting majors as a foundation for the required upper-division accounting courses (ACC 250).

The primary goals of the introductory accounting sequence are to (1) expose all students to the multiple uses and limitations of accounting information and (2) prepare the accounting majors for subsequent accounting courses. The new introductory accounting sequence was successfully implemented during the 1992-93 academic year.

Information Systems Foundation for Upper-Division Accounting Courses

The first accounting course taken by accounting majors after the introductory accounting sequence is Accounting Information Systems (ACC 330). This course includes modules on (1) accounting information systems overview, (2) transaction processing, (3) information technology, (4) user-oriented decision support, and (5) system development life cycle. External reporting, internal reporting, taxation and auditing are viewed as subsystems of the overall information system.

The accounting information systems course is a prerequisite for all other upper-division accounting courses and provides the information systems knowledge and some of the technical skills needed for those courses. The new accounting information systems course was implemented during the first semester of the 1993-94 academic year.

Increased Use of the Case Method

To develop our students' ability to analyze more complex and unstructured problems, the case method was integrated into all upper division accounting courses. Many MBA programs and selected advanced undergraduate business and accounting courses have used the case method successfully. The case method forces students to become more involved in the learning process, and it exposes them to real world problems, many of which are relatively unstructured. Students must learn to apply theories and concepts to problems that may not have "textbook" solutions.

Under the case method of instruction, students are active participants in the learning process, which should increase the level of learning achieved. The case method encourages students to learn to learn, which is more important in the long run than memorizing rules, definitions and procedures.

Adoption of Cooperative Learning/Active Learning Pedagogy

Cooperative learning is a highly structured form of small group work that is based on positive interdependence, individual accountability, heterogeneous teams, group processing and social skills. Research has shown that cooperative learning has positive effects on student achievement, multiethnic relationships, self-esteem, student retention and student attitudes. A sense of community and cooperation is promoted by this learner-centered pedagogy. This approach to student learning was used to transform our classrooms into active learning environments with students fully engaged in the learning process.

Our new introductory accounting sequence relies heavily on cooperative learning activities. The results to date have been very positive and encouraging. Most students want to be actively involved in the learning process versus being a spectator. This approach is also used in our upper-division accounting courses. Our graduates will have extensive experience working in teams to solve challenging problems.

Incorporation of Laboratory Science Format
for Upper-Division Accounting Courses

A typical laboratory science course at a semester-system university is a four credit-hour course involving three hours per week in a classroom and three hours per week in a laboratory. The physical sciences have used this approach successfully for several decades as the laboratory experience is an integral component of most physical science courses. The laboratory provides "hands on" experience for the students to reinforce the concepts discussed in the classroom meetings. This format is used for all six upper-division accounting courses.

To increase the amount of time available to discuss cases in the classroom and to use more time-intensive teaching methods such as cooperative learning, some traditional in-class activities was transferred to the labs. For example, much of the mechanical and procedural material was transferred to the lab, and often computer-based instruction was used to cover this material. In addition, examinations and quizzes were given in the labs, thereby increasing the time available for professor/student and student/student interaction in the classroom. Video tapes were used to introduce new material or to provide important background information to facilitate classroom discussion. The students view the tapes in the lab, and discuss and debate relevant issues in the classroom. The lab format also facilitated the use of outside speakers as needed in our upper-division classes.

Accounting Program Summary

Accounting majors are required to take six upper-division accounting courses. Each course uses the lab science format, cooperative/active learning pedagogy and the case method. Students complete accounting information systems (ACC 330) prior to courses involving external reporting (ACC 340 and ACC 440), internal reporting (ACC 350), taxation (ACC 430) and auditing (ACC 450) or a second course in internal reporting (ACC 494).

Each course builds on the accounting knowledge and skills acquired in previous courses. For example, the accounting information systems course provides a foundation for the five accounting courses that follow and provides accountancy majors with an information systems perspective of the accounting discipline.

Methods of Achieving Faculty and Administrative Support

The support of the accounting faculty was gradually obtained during the development of our proposal. The leadership of the Director of the SOA, influence of the Bedford Committee Report and the Big 8 White Paper, input from the SOA Professional Advisory Board, the possibility of funding from the AECC, support of the College Dean and University President, and numerous faculty meetings all played a crucial role in gaining the near unanimous support of the accounting faculty. Administrative support was fortunately much easier to obtain. Both the newly appointed President of ASU and the Dean of the College of Business were strong advocates for excellence in undergraduate education.

Change Activities That Worked Well and Which Others Might Copy

Our AECC project included five successful major innovations that represented significant departures from the prior accounting program. It would be possible for other schools to use any or all of these innovations. The five innovations, discussed in a prior section, were:

1. Restructure of the introductory accounting sequence.
2. Accounting information systems as the first upper division accounting course.

3. Significant increase in use of the case method.
4. Emphasis on active/cooperative learning pedagogies.
5. Use of lab science format for upper-division accounting courses.

Restructure of the introductory accounting sequence

Our very traditional financial accounting/managerial accounting introductory sequence was successfully restructured into three accounting courses. The first two, ACC 230 and ACC 240, emphasize the uses and limitations of accounting information and are required of all business majors. Both courses have a user orientation, and traditional preparation skills are not covered. Each course meets once a week in a large classroom using an interactive lecture approach and once or twice a week in smaller break-out sections that use cooperative learning activities. The third course in the revised sequence, ACC 250, focuses solely on the traditional preparation skills needed by accounting majors for the upper-division financial accounting courses. ACC 250 is required of all accounting majors and is normally taken during the first semester of the junior year. This course is taught almost entirely on the computer using courseware developed by the SOA. The development of the courseware for ACC 250 was very labor-intensive. Not all schools would have the resources needed to develop this courseware. Fortunately for those who would like to use this approach, the courseware is available through Irwin/McGraw-Hill. The accounting team (R. Smith, Jones, Birney, Davis, Doran, Drieke, Weaver and Weber) that was responsible for the restructure of the introductory accounting sequence received the 1995 American Accounting Association Award for Innovations in Accounting Education.

Accounting information systems as the first upper division accounting course

This change, while consistent with the recommendations of the Bedford Committee, was probably the most controversial of the changes made. The traditional accounting education model emphasized the financial accounting sequence and in particular the intermediate accounting courses as being the most important accounting courses. Under this model, students tended to view accounting rather narrowly. Accounting to many students was debits and credits, journal entries and GAAP; that is, financial accounting. It was deemed important that students see the bigger picture of accounting information systems without diminishing the important role of financial accounting. Accounting information systems is a prerequisite for all upper-division accounting courses (internal reporting, external reporting, taxes and business decisions, and auditing).

Significant increase in use of the case method

Cases and the case method have been used to expose our students to real world problems (versus the more structured textbook problems), and to practice a solution technique that should be useful for any accounting career alternative that is selected. It has been our experience that (1) accounting undergraduates are very capable of analyzing cases, and (2) unstructured problem solving skills are enhanced from this activity. It would be relatively easy for any school or accounting instructor to integrate cases and the case method into courses in the accounting curriculum.

Emphasis on active/cooperative learning pedagogies

The use of highly structured group work (cooperative learning) has greatly facilitated the attainment of many of our AECC project goals. The benefits of cooperative learning are well documented. Accounting students are not allowed to passively observe what goes on in our classes. They are now active participants in the learning process and, accordingly, long-tern retention should be enhanced. In addition, their interpersonal, team and communications skills should be strengthened. The accounting classroom has been transformed into an active learning environment, and the accounting instructor has assumed the additional role of a facilitator and manager of the learning process. With the appropriate training, any accounting instructor could successfully use the cooperative learning approach. However, this pedagogy is not as simple to use as the traditional lecture method. It requires significant time and effort on the part of the instructor and support of a cooperative learning expert.

Use of lab science format for upper-division accounting courses

As a result of the Bedford Committee Report and the Big 8 White Paper, accounting instructors were being asked to be responsible for more than just accounting technical skills. Several non-accounting skills (communication, interpersonal, etc.) were not being adequately developed by our students. Most accounting faculty did not want to sacrifice accounting technical skills to gain the important non-accounting skills. In addition, two of the new pedagogies (the case method and cooperative learning) were considered to be relatively time-intensive approaches. It was obvious that we could not fit all of this into the traditional three-hour courses that we had. We needed more contact hours with our students to accomplish our goals. The lab science format was used to gain the additional hours. Each of the six upper-division accounting courses is now four credit hours and consists of three hours in a small class setting with the regular accounting professor and three hours in a common lab for all sections of the same course. The lab is staffed by a combination of accounting faculty, doctoral students and other graduate students. The lab format has been successful in providing the additional hours needed to address the requested non-accounting skills and more time-intensive pedagogies.

For example, in ACC 340 (Internal Reporting I), students first attempt to solve the assigned cases, exercises, or problems (lab activities) independently prior to the lab session. Subsequently, they join their groups to work cooperatively on the lab activities during the lab session. If the group as a whole cannot solve a specific lab activity, the next step is to request guidance from one of the lab assistants. The lab assistants are guides whose questions, promptings and insertions of information support the students' understanding of the lab activities. Early lab sessions in ACC 340 are more structured and directed until students become accustomed to working in their groups with lab assistants as resources. The lab sessions emphasize excellence in contrast to remediation. The students are actively involved in the learning process in the ACC 340 and other accounting labs.

Change Activities Undertaken That Did Not Work

There were some changes that were made that either had to be modified or still are in the process of modification. For example, ACC 250 was originally offered on a (high) pass/fail grading basis. After the first year, we changed the course to a regular grade basis. Also, we originally suggested that students take ACC 250 during the second semester of their sophomore year. To minimize the time gap between this course and the first upper-division financial accounting course (ACC 340), ACC 250 is now recommended for the first semester of the junior year. In addition, a practice set has been added to the beginning of ACC 340 to enhance the procedural skills needed for the external reporting courses (ACC 340 and ACC 440).

The use of the lab format has been successful in some courses and not so successful in others. Developing value-added learning activities for the labs has been a significant challenge that has not been solved in some classes. In addition, the common labs have caused some scheduling problems, and the university has few rooms available that are adequate for our labs. At present, all the labs are on Fridays with several in the afternoon to avoid scheduling conflicts and to secure appropriate rooms. Often there is a significant noise problem in some labs due to the poor acoustics of the rooms that are being used. Some of these classrooms are scheduled for renovation in the near future and hopefully will become adequate for our needs. The scheduling problems continue to be addressed.

In addition to ACC 250, computer technology has been used in other accounting courses to supplement the learning process. The courseware that was developed initially was for a network application. Effective Fall 1994, the university switched to a new network system. Since then, there have been constant problems for many of the computer-related activities. As a result of the network problems and suggestions from schools without adequate networks wanting to use the ACC 250 courseware, portable (take-home) versions of the courseware have been developed and continue to be developed. The portable version will offset many, but not all, of the network problems encountered. For the faculty involved in the development and testing of this courseware, the network problems were extremely frustrating.

Students do not like group grades! They like learning in groups, but they want to be evaluated individually. One of the essential elements of cooperative learning is individual accountability. In some instances, the increased use of group grades created some situations that over the years have given group work a bad reputation. Cooperative learning does not require group grades. If you use group grades, proceed with caution.

Unexpected Benefits From Change Activities

There were several unexpected benefits from going through the change process. Our AECC grant proposal did not mention cooperative learning. We discovered this pedagogy during the initial phases of the change process. Based on our goals and objectives, cooperative learning was a very appropriate pedagogy to employ in our courses. In addition, the level of student camaraderie has increased significantly. Student to student contact has increased significantly as a result of the group activities. One of the common complaints about group work, especially where many students work part-time, is that they cannot find a time to meet outside of class. The labs can provide time for students to do a significant amount of their group work.

One of the cooperative learning activities that produced positive results was the use of individual quizzes followed by the same quiz taken by the group. This activity increased the level of preparation for class partly because of peer pressure, and provided opportunities for students to explain (teach) and justify their answers to their group members. This is a relatively simple technique to use and has produced positive results.

The courseware that has been developed for several courses extends far beyond our most ambitious dreams of what was possible for us in this area. We wanted to make use of computer technology to enhance the learning process, and feel that we have vastly exceeded our expectations in this area. As a spin-off of the ACC 250 courseware, similar efforts have been completed for intermediate and managerial accounting. In addition, courseware was developed for the tax and auditing courses. Our students like the instant feedback provided by the courseware. For at least a part of the course we are able to simulate a one-to-one learning environment for our students. The accounting instructors can review the results of how well the students have done on their homework prior to each class, and can then better plan their usage of class time.

Because of the changes made in accounting, some faculty in other departments in the college have started to make changes in their courses. For example, several have incorporated cooperative learning and/or computer technology in their courses. In addition, the Dean has encouraged faculty to consider more active learning techniques such as cooperative learning.

As a result of the change process, we have received several local and national awards: the previously mentioned AAA Award for Innovations in Accounting Education as well as the (ASU) President's Award and Governor's Award for Team Excellence. ASU has started a series to feature curriculum innovations within the university. The School of Accountancy was asked to make the first presentation in this series. In addition, we have made numerous presentations at local, regional and national accounting meetings.

Measurement of the Effects of Changes Accomplished

The School of Accountancy assesses the effectiveness and productivity of its undergraduate program using a multitude of evaluations. The objective of the assessment program is to measure and document the achievement of the SOA learning goals for the undergraduate program and to facilitate a continuous improvement process. A brief description of each assessment activity follows.

SURVEYS/QUESTIONNAIRES:

Survey of Employers/Recruiters. Twenty-three firms that actively recruit our graduates have been asked to respond to a mail survey that measures (1) how effectively our graduates meet thirteen objectives established for our program, and (2) how our current graduates compare to prior ASU graduates. This survey was administered for the first time during May 1995 and will be repeated annually.

Student Surveys. All accounting majors were asked to respond to a survey during Spring 1995 to measure their perceptions of how successful our new program is in terms of meeting its program objectives. This survey will be repeated each semester.

SOA Supplemental Learning Assessment. The SOA developed a questionnaire to be administered in all upper-division required accounting courses to evaluate (1) learning of accounting-related skills and abilities, (2) effectiveness of cooperative learning, (3) attainment of instructional objectives, and (4) the effectiveness of the accounting labs. This questionnaire was used for the first time during the Fall 1994 and will be repeated each semester.

Graduating Senior Survey. The ASU Office of Evaluation surveys graduating seniors annually concerning the overall quality of the college experience. The School of Accountancy receives detailed results of this survey for the accountancy majors that participate.

1987-88 Graduates Survey. In 1994, the ASU Office of Evaluation surveyed 1987-88 graduates to gather perceptions about their college experiences. The SOA designed a special four-page insert for accounting majors who were surveyed. This survey will be repeated when our first new program graduates have been out of school for a similar period of time.

COB Standard Teaching Evaluation Form. A standard student evaluation form is used to evaluate instruction in all COB courses. The evaluations for accounting classes are reviewed by the SOA Director and the appropriate Associate Dean and are returned to the instructor. Numerous teaching awards have been won by faculty and doctoral students in the SOA.

FSA Annual Survey of Accounting Graduates/Majors. The FSA Data Base Committee conducts an annual survey of accounting graduates at member institutions. The purpose of this survey is to gather information that "will help accounting educators and professionals develop strategies for identifying and attracting talented, high-quality students to the accounting profession."

TESTS/EXAMINATIONS:

ACT Standardized Exam for Critical Thinking. To assess the critical thinking skills of our students, a standardized exam from ACT has been administered first to graduates of our old program (1993) and more recently to graduates of our new program (1995). The Critical Thinking Test is a 40 minute, 32 item test that measures the ability to clarify, analyze, evaluate and extend arguments.

ACT Standardized Exam for Writing. To assess the writing skills of our students, a standardized exam from ACT has been administered first to graduates of our old program (1993) and more recently to graduates of our new program (1995). The Writing (Essay) Test consists of two 20-minute writing tasks defined by a specific hypothetical situation and audience that tests basic writing skills.

Defining Issues Test. The DIT evaluates an individual's moral judgment and development. This test was administered to 120 seniors during Spring 1994 to establish a baseline measurement and was repeated in 1996 to see if the new accounting program has resulted in significant improvements.

AICPA Achievement Test for Accounting Graduates. This standardized examination includes multiple choice items in the following areas: financial accounting, managerial accounting, accounting information systems, taxation and auditing. This examination was given to graduates of our old program and was repeated in 1996 to assess any change in accounting technical skills.

Performance on the CPA Examination. While passing the CPA Examination is not a stated objective of the new accounting program, performance on the CPA Examination can be used as a crude indicator of any changes in technical competence in accounting of our graduates.

Individual Course Exams. To document accounting and related skills, course examinations are an integral part of every accounting course. These examinations are used both to evaluate student performance and to continuously improve the efficiency and effectiveness of the teaching/learning process.

OTHER ASSESSMENTS:

Student/Faculty Assessment Luncheons. All students in our final accounting course (ACC 450) were invited to share their views, both positive and negative, of our new program with faculty and administrators not directly involved in teaching the new courses. These assessment luncheons will be repeated each year. The sessions were audio taped and a transcript was prepared.

Course Syllabus Matrix. Periodically, an activities matrix will be constructed to document the number of writing assignments, the number of oral presentations, the number of cases used, the number of ethics assignments, etc. that are included in the upper-division accounting courses. The results of this analysis will help to identify areas where coverage of various skills needs to be modified.

Special Insights From Carrying Out AECC Grant

Faculty clearly prefer an evolutionary change process even when a revolutionary change process is needed. Faculty in general may be more resistant to change than any other group. Academic freedom may be used as an excuse not to change or to work in teams. University faculty tend to operate as independent contractors. As a general rule, we get to teach what we want to teach when we want teach it, and get to research whatever we want to research. If we want to work with others, we can, but it is not required. Very rarely have we been in situations where we have had to compromise and not have it our way. The change process required consensus and compromise which was difficult for many. We found sometimes that our team skills were not adequate.

Unfortunately, we found out that some (a minority) of our students did not want the new and improved accounting program if it meant more effort on their part and/or change on their part. These students were eager at times to "badmouth" the changes to anyone who would listen. The negativity was not limited to our undergraduate students. Fortunately, this negativity was overwhelmed by the enthusiastic support of our dean, the employers who hire our graduates, and our professional advisory board, as well as most of our accounting faculty. It still was disappointing to encounter those who did not share our enthusiasm.

Plans to Perpetuate the Changes That Worked Well

The assessment process has started, but is not complete as to the ultimate success of our major curriculum changes. The preliminary evidence is very encouraging, but the continuous improvement process requires constant evaluation. All of the new courses have received the appropriate faculty and administrative approvals and are in the university catalog. The supporting pedagogies will continue until there is evidence that a change needs to be made. The SOA has an assessment team that is charged with this activity. The new AACSB guidelines require a continuous improvement process. Though the time period covered by our AECC grant recently ended, the SOA, in response to market factors, has made another significant curriculum change. Effective Fall 1996, accountancy majors are required to complete nine hours of computer information systems courses as a part of the business core.

Dissemination of Results of AECC Grant Activities

The primary means used to disseminate the results of our curriculum development project have been numerous presentations at local, regional and national meetings of accounting educators. For example, our three most active presenters (Jones, Birney and McKenzie) have made collectively in excess of 100 presentations.

Materials Available and How to Obtain

The courseware that was developed for ACC 250 and several other accounting courses is available through Irwin/McGraw-Hill. The ACC 230/240 text that resulted from this project (*Introduction to Financial Accounting: A User Perspective* by Kumen Jones, Jean Price, Michael Werner and Martha Doran) is available from Prentice-Hall.

A current course syllabus and related materials for all revised accounting courses is available via internet: http://www.cob.asu.edu/acct/aecc/aecc.html

For additional information, contact School of Accountancy and Information Management, College of Business, Arizona State University, Tempe, AZ 85287-3606 or telephone (602) 965-3631.

Chapter 2
BRIGHAM YOUNG UNIVERSITY
Integrated Junior Year Accounting Core

Type, Size and Mission of Accounting Program

The mission of the School of Accountancy & Information Systems (SOAIS) at BYU is to achieve excellence in accounting and information systems education and to cultivate a passion for life-long learning, founded on the values of The Church of Jesus Christ of Latter-day Saints (Mormons). BYU does not offer a Ph.D. in accounting or business. Since 1976, students have applied to and entered the accounting program at the beginning of their junior year with the option of continuing for two years and receiving a Bachelor of Science (B.S.) degree, or continuing for three years and simultaneously receiving a B.S. and Master of Accountancy (MAcc) degrees. Currently, approximately 260 students are admitted at the beginning of the junior year from a qualified applicant pool of approximately 360 students. Approximately 160 students are allowed to continue on into the masters program from a qualified applicant pool of over 250 students (approximately 200 BYU undergraduates and 50 B.S. degree holders from the outside).

Students entering the SOAIS are screened for admission three times: (1) admission to BYU (3.7 average high school GPA, 27.0 ACT), (2) admission to the Marriott School of Management (MSM) (700 students admitted annually with a 3.4 BYU GPA), and (3) admission to the SOAIS (3.62 average BYU GPA). The BYU student body is cosmopolitan, including students from all 50 states and approximately 70 foreign countries. Most students have served two-year foreign missions for the Mormon church and, as a result, speak fluently a second language.

Characteristics of Program Before the Grant

Although SOAIS graduates were being well received in the marketplace, the faculty recognized in the curriculum and courses some of the criticism frequently leveled against accounting education. For example, too often students were required to memorize IRS code sections or FASB pronouncements. Many faculty relied primarily on the lecture method of instruction to cover the rapidly expanding body of knowledge. Assignments were often limited to textbook problems with one "right answer." In many courses, especially at the undergraduate level, instructors did not allow time for students to explore the conceptual foundation and real-world relevance of accounting information. Professors encouraged writing skills in several courses, but not in all, with oral communication skills emphasized only at the graduate level. Students did not participate in extensive group work in most classes. In addition, there was a lack of program continuity, as courses were treated as separate entities with little or no interaction among professors of different courses and functional specializations.

Central Objective of Grant

BYU's AECC project had three goals: (1) to identify the competencies needed by professional accountants in the next decade, (2) to design a curriculum that would develop those competencies in students, and (3) to assess the effectiveness of the new curriculum in achieving the desired competencies.

To meet the first goal, identifying needed competencies, a field survey was conducted of 873 practicing CPAs in Southern California and accountants within the Marriott and Phillips Petroleum companies. From this survey and a careful review of other literature, 27 competencies were identified. (See Deppe, et al 1991, p. 278).

To meet the second goal, designing a curriculum that would cultivate the needed competencies, faculty efforts focused on two types of changes: (1) changes in the overall structure of the accounting program, and (2) changes in the curriculum and pedagogy within the junior year.

To meet the third goal, assessing the effectiveness of the changed program, formative evaluation was conducted as the program was being designed and implemented and summative evaluation was conducted once the curriculum was in place. An educational consultant aided accounting faculty in gathering data throughout the restructuring process. Through formative evaluations, adjustments to the program were made continually. Through summative evaluation, attempts have been made to capture the impact of the new program on students, faculty, and external parties.

Key Means of Accomplishing Grant Objective

Even before the grant was received, an SOAIS Faculty Task Force began meeting biweekly to consider changes to the SOAIS curriculum. Initial discussions were limited to suggestions of moving existing courses from the junior year to the senior year or vice-versa. Once the grant was received, the task force decided to focus on the competencies identified in the survey research, the Bedford Committee report, and the Perspectives "white paper," and to identify a suitable curriculum for developing these competencies. A faculty member from the College of Education was recruited to assist the task force in defining pedagogical deficiencies and in framing an approach to changing the curriculum.

A team of 12 full-time faculty members developed the revised curriculum, two each from the functional areas of tax, financial accounting, managerial accounting, systems, and auditing, along with a law professor and an international accounting professor. The 12 faculty included a wide range of age and experience, a factor that provided a needed balance to the changes that were made and increased the acceptability of the recommendations. These 12 faculty taught the new program during the first year. Another seven faculty members were added to the teaching team in the second year with several more added the third year.

Department, college, and university administrators supported the change efforts by supplying release time and supplemental financial grants to faculty members who worked on the project. BYU's administration and faculty have traditionally emphasized the importance of teaching, providing a fertile environment for significant curriculum change.

Major Changes from Pre-Grant Conditions

AECC changes focused primarily on the junior year. The accounting topics of intermediate accounting, cost/managerial accounting, tax, auditing, law, and systems had been taught traditionally as separate functional courses. The faculty decided to combine these courses into an integrated, team-taught, 24 semester-credit-hour core. This core encompassed traditional content competencies and also nine "expanded" or skill-based competencies identified in the survey research. The faculty selected the business cycle approach, a methodology proven successful in auditing and systems courses, as a paradigm to introduce the various topics. This new structure is consistent with the Bedford Committee's recommendation that accounting should be taught as part of a total information system.

With this revised structure, students attend the junior core three hours a day, four days a week for two sequential academic semesters (fall and winter). In addition, students typically register for one non-core course each semester. During the first ten weeks of the core, students are introduced to certain "foundation" topics in each of the functional areas, including the conceptual framework in financial accounting; the audit risk model, internal control and evidence accumulation in auditing; basic concepts in corporate taxation and law; and business-event systems concepts, including introduction to a relational database in systems. The foundation phases includes instruction on how to research issues and find answers in the professional accounting, auditing, and tax literature. During this period, students are introduced to NAARS, NEXIS, LEXIS and other electronic databases and given assignments requiring them to use these sources.

After the foundation phase, five business cycles form the framework for teaching the technical and expanded competencies: (1) sales/collection, (2) acquisition/payment, (3) payroll/performance evaluation, (4) conversion/inventory, and (5) financing. This framework increases efficiency in presentation and discussion. For example, inventory topics are traditionally covered in intermediate accounting, managerial accounting, tax, auditing, and to some extent, systems, with each course considering inventory from a different perspective and user view. The business cycle framework enables students to consider all aspects of inventory at the same time and facilitates discussion of different perspectives on the same issue. The following diagram graphically outlines the integrated structure of the new program.

Freshman & Sophomore Years

Students complete general education requirements and take pre-business and pre-accounting requirements including introductory accounting, calculus, statistics, economics and business communications. Approximately 260 students are admitted to the SOAIS at the conclusion of the sophomore year.

Junior Year

SOAIS students are enrolled in the integrated, team-taught core that meets for three hours, four days a week during the entire year. The junior year is divided into four grading blocks, each consisting of six semester hours of credit. Teams of five professors from the functional areas of systems, financial accounting, managerial accounting, tax, and auditing, plus law and international accounting professors, team teach sections of approximately 60 students each. At the end of the year, students apply for the five-year, master of accountancy program (MAcc) or elect to graduate with a four-year bachelor's degree.

Senior Year, 1st Semester

The 160 SOAIS students who are accepted into the MAcc program participate in another team-taught, three-hour per day, integrated program that is taken by all business graduate students including MBAs. Professors from the functional areas of business management, finance, marketing, organizational behavior, strategy, and communications teach integrated sections of 50-60 students each. Students who elect a bachelor's degree or who are not admitted to the 150-hour program take undergraduate, non-accounting business courses and other electives.

Senior Year, 2nd Semester

MAcc students begin to specialize in information systems, tax, pre Ph.D., or professional accounting by taking specialty courses in those areas as well as business and non-business electives. Bachelor's students complete their degrees by taking other undergraduate business and elective courses.

Fifth Year

MAcc students continue specialization in tax, pre Ph.D., professional accounting or information systems. Graduates receive master's and bachelor's degrees simultaneously at the end of the year.

Methods of Achieving Faculty
and Administrative Support for Changes

The decision to apply for the AECC grant was only made after a unanimous vote of the entire faculty. We were united in our desire to be instigators and leaders of change rather than followers. Once faculty unity was achieved, the administration was approached. Because BYU has always valued and rewarded high-quality teaching, both the Dean and university supported applying for the grant. Once the grant was awarded, we requested and received a "letter of agreement" from the University President stating that curriculum change projects and related work would be considered scholarship and that publications resulting from curriculum work would be considered as "research publications" for evaluation purposes. It also helped to engage a highly respected faculty member in Instructional Science, who endorsed and assisted with the project. He provided comfort to the university administration that our changes were positive and would improve our already highly respected accounting program.

Change Activities That Worked Well and Which Others Might Copy

Our AECC project included eight curriculum and pedagogical innovations that worked well. While all eight were integrated simultaneously into the BYU curriculum, they are largely separable, and any or all of them can be used at other schools. These eight innovations are:
1. Integrating expanded competency instruction with content instruction.
2. Organizing and integrating technical content by business cycles.
3. Using new teaching approaches, including extensive use of student groups (cooperative learning) and teaching in three-hour blocks.
4. Grading on the basis of both technical and skill-based competencies.
5. Using a business-events systems approach to teaching accounting.
6. Using a faculty team approach to planning, teaching and evaluation.
7. Developing detailed teaching plans for each class period.
8. Using textbooks and other materials as resources rather than as drivers of the curriculum.

Integrating Expanded Competencies

Phase I of our AECC project identified 27 competencies needed by accounting professionals. At least seven of the competencies were content based, requiring that students gain knowledge in accounting, auditing, tax, and business. Most of the other competencies were skill based (expanded) and were not previously included explicitly in the accounting curriculum. The faculty decided to focus on nine skill-based competencies in addition to the content competencies. The nine competencies can be grouped into five categories as follows:

Written Communication:
1.   Ability to present views in writing.
Oral Communication:
2.   Ability to present views through oral communication.
3.   Ability to listen effectively.
Group Work and People Skills:
4.   Ability to understand group dynamics and work effectively with people.
5.   Ability to resolve conflict.
6.   Ability to organize and delegate tasks.
Critical Thinking:
7.   Ability to solve diverse and unstructured problems.
8.   Ability to read, critique, and judge the value of written work.
Working Under Pressure:
9.   Ability to deal effectively with imposed pressure and deadlines.

As the new curriculum was developed, these nine expanded competencies became part of the focus of each day's planning. Each three-hour block emphasized one or more of these competencies, as well as technical content. Grading was designed to weight content and expanded competencies equally.

Organizing and Integrating Technical Content by Business Cycles

Before the restructuring, BYU's program might have been characterized as a series of stovepipes. Tax, auditing, financial accounting, managerial accounting, law, and systems were taught in separate courses, with little attempt to integrate topical matter.

It was decided early in the planning process that the new program would integrate content across functional areas rather than teaching separate courses. All accounting topics now taught in the junior year are integrated throughout the year in their appropriate business cycle. Organizing content around business cycles has been one of the most popular aspects of the new curriculum for students, faculty, and outside observers. Topics that were previously fragmented into several different classes are now covered once, in detail, with an opportunity for integrated understanding. Case material and other assignments often cover a number of different topical areas.

Using New Teaching Approaches

In designing the new curriculum, the faculty realized that new teaching approaches would be required to replace much of the previous lecture format, which would not adapt well to teaching many of the expanded competencies. The integrated structure of the core, as well as the three-hour time blocks, allowed many different and creative pedagogies.

The significant use of groups in and out of the classroom altered the focus of many class sessions from the teacher to the students. Examinations, written and oral, were created to evaluate critical thinking skills as well as content knowledge. Faculty members experimented with many different teaching strategies and used student feedback as well as faculty peer comments to evaluate the different pedagogical approaches.

Some approaches were not well received, some case assignments were not useful, and some in-class student assignments were not effective and have been discontinued. In every case where changes were made, the acid test was not how difficult the concept was to teach or learn, but rather how effective the pedagogy was. Students willingly participated in providing constant feedback to faculty.

Grading on the Basis of Both Technical and Skill-Based Competencies

One of the most difficult administrative decisions faced in restructuring the program was determining the methods to grade the expanded and technical competencies. In order to evaluate communication skills, group activities, ability to work with unstructured problems and other expanded competencies, the faculty had to solve two problems: (1) how to evaluate the more subjective skill-based competencies in view of the lack of faculty experience in these types of evaluations, and (2) how to aggregate separate competency evaluations into a single course grade.

In dealing with the first problem, faculty focused on each of the nine expanded competencies, identifying student activities that would demonstrate proficiency in each area and could be graded. The faculty selected several of these assignments for each cycle and incorporated them into the teaching plans.

In dealing with the second problem, the faculty experimented with different methods of determining course grades. Students and faculty finally decided that the most fair system was to establish grade cut-offs that produced a grade point average of 3.4 from a distribution of all 260 student scores. The grades produced by this system were lower than the incoming student averages, but higher than had been typical in the pre-change curriculum.

Using a Business Events System Approach to Teaching Accounting

The concept of accounting information being part of a total information system used by business is the framework around which the junior year core was designed. This approach allowed the curriculum to focus on the role that accounting plays in the decision processes of management. During the foundation phase, students were trained in the use of spreadsheets and relational database. They were also introduced to concepts of systems design and data modeling, and were trained to use a business events framework, as well as the traditional double-entry system of accounting. The systems faculty introduced each of the five business cycles and included a careful study of the external and internal agents and resources involved with the cycle. They also covered the systems characteristics that would best capture the key information concerning these events. Each of the other functional areas then built their teaching plans on the systems foundation of each cycle.

Using a Faculty Team Approach to Planning, Teaching, and Evaluation
     After obtaining the AECC grant, 12 accounting professors met weekly for eight months, jointly developing 112 teaching plans for the core. Once the semester began, faculty held weekly meetings to discuss grading, assignments, coordination, teaching plans, and outcome measurements. Where possible, professors from different functional areas team-taught integrated topics.
     Team planning and teaching had significant advantages. One benefit was the significant cross-training that occurred as faculty learned about functional areas other than their own. In addition, faculty shared ideas and preferences about grading, administration, and other teaching support functions that had not been discussed openly in the past. Faculty unity increased through these weekly planning sessions.

Developing Detailed Teaching Plans for Each Class
     The team-taught, competency-based curriculum founded on a systems approach required coordination among faculty. Faculty had to agree on which topics would be included in each cycle, the class time that would be allowed for each topic and functional area, pre- and post-class assignments, skill-based competencies to be covered, and professors to be involved. Students needed to know what was expected each day.
     To facilitate this coordination, the faculty developed common teaching plans. The professors used the teaching plans to ensure consistency across sections and instructors. Students used the teaching plans to prepare for each class session. Each day's teaching plan included the following elements:
*   BUSINESS CYCLE and DATE of instruction.
*   FUNCTIONAL TOPICS being covered.
*   COMPETENCY FOCUS. (The expanded competencies which were emphasized in the teaching pedagogy.)
*   CONTENT LEARNING OBJECTIVES.
*   EXPANDED COMPETENCY LEARNING OBJECTIVES. (Behavioral learning objectives related to the expanded competencies.)
*   PRE-CLASS ASSIGNMENT. (Reading, written, oral and group assignments for the current class period.)
*   POST-CLASS ASSIGNMENT. (Assignments for the next and future class periods.)
In addition to the items included on the teaching plans distributed to students, faculty teaching plans also described the class format, with approximate time to be allocated to each class activity and the evaluation methods designed for each competency and technical skill. These teaching plans, with accompanying supplemental material, became the basis for student packets that were sold to students for each six-hour block.

Using Textbooks and Other Materials as Resources Rather than as Drivers of the Curriculum
     Most accounting courses require textbooks that serve as both a resource and a driver of activities. Topical material usually follows the sequence presented in the

textbook. The problems and exercises used for homework and examinations are most often derived from textbook material. Since content in the new curriculum was presented in the sequence of business cycles, and functional areas were integrated, traditional textbooks could not drive course organization or class structure. Although each functional area required textbooks, they served as only one of a number of reading sources for the different topical areas. Professor-created and commercial cases and other materials were also used.

In addition to textbooks and cases, the curriculum involves extensive use of current readings from *The Wall Street Journal, Business Week, Forbes, Fortune,* and other periodicals. Required readings from current business periodicals provided current applications for the topics being discussed, and ensured relevance of the education process.

Change Activities Undertaken That Did Not Work

Although almost all changes were positive, faculty did express concern about a number of factors: (1) the loss of autonomy and control in the classroom, (2) the lack of individual ownership of courses, (3) the labor intensiveness of the program, (4) a possible reduction in the amount of technical knowledge being learned by students, and (5) the necessity of teaching in front of colleagues in a team-teaching environment. In addition, we still face several critical challenges as we move forward.

1. Some students are forced to discontinue their schooling for short periods of time. Because of the integrated nature of the program, it is difficult to stop in midstream and start again. Presently, classes are being videotaped and stored in the library for student viewing. Longer-term absences are very difficult to deal with.

2. Teaching in the core and focusing on expanded competencies requires significantly more faculty time than does self-contained learning. Because university, college and department faculty evaluation criteria, which govern rank advancement, promotion, and tenure require publication, faculty may consider the cost of involvement as too high. Presently, curriculum development and teaching activities at BYU are recognized and rewarded. If those rewards cease, faculty may decide the new curriculum is not worth the extra effort.

3. The tendency exists to intersperse topics rather than integrate them. The most effective integration takes place when faculty members sit in on each other's classes or participate frequently in sharing class-time in a true team-teaching mode. When faculty just attend class on "their days," and ignore other faculty presentations, little integration takes place. Students are becoming much more integrated than are faculty.

4. The junior year core is more expensive than traditional, lecture-based classes. Additional teaching assistants and graders are necessary, and faculty must have

time for additional preparation if the program is to succeed. Added costs for video and multi-media presentations are also incurred. Decreases in funding may force administrators and faculty to question the incremental value of the more expensive curriculum.

5. Faculty need more opportunities to strengthen their professional knowledge and skills. The integrated core is demanding, and faculty knowledge must be current and extensive. In addition to their specific areas of expertise, faculty must better understand the academic content being covered by other faculty members. Faculty development is time consuming and expensive.

6. Policies need to be established concerning transfer students coming to BYU from other institutions. Presently transfer students can only be accepted at the beginning of the junior year core or after completing B.S. degrees at other schools. Non-degree students transferring into the program after having taken part of their degree requirements at another school must wait for the fall entry point and enroll in the entire curriculum with other beginning students. If applicant numbers ever decrease, these transfer policies may need modification.

Unexpected Benefits

Several unexpected benefits have come to the SOAIS because of the curriculum changes made. The quality of students applying to the accounting programs has increased substantially. BYU students now say, "let's apply to the accounting program," not "let's take an accounting class." Accounting has developed a reputation on campus much like law and the MBA program. Second, recruiters are competing much more intensely for our graduates. Recruiters like and support our curriculum and nearly all graduates are being placed through our campus recruiting, usually in excellent jobs. One Big Six firm has hired 112 students during the past two years. A third unexpected benefit has been the increased respect for the SOAIS from university administrators. The SOAIS has been identified by the university President as the "strongest unit on campus." Fourth, contributions to the SOAIS have increased substantially since making curriculum changes. Two major donors have given money to the SOAIS because of their enthusiasm for what we are now doing and the respect the program has achieved nationwide.

Measurement of the Effects of Changes Accomplished

As mentioned earlier, formative and summative evaluation procedures were conducted during and after the AECC project. Formative measures (established during development) include:

Formative Measures of Success
1. Feedback from students on a daily basis.
    A. What was the most important thing you learned today?
    B. What wasn't clear?
    C. How helpful were in-class and out-of-class assignments and activities?
2. Feedback received during weekly brown bag sessions with students.
3. Class video tapes by faculty and others.
4. Discussions during weekly planning and evaluation meetings by faculty involved.
5. Feedback during small-group socials in faculty homes.
6. Notes and journals kept by professors about successes and failures.
7. Feedback from teaching assistants who were hired to observe and evaluate classes.
8. Discussions during periodic retreats which were held to discuss the program.
9. Student scores on tests during the year.
10. Assessments of the quality of student presentations, written work, and other assignments by communication faculty and others.

Summative Assessment Measures — End of the First Year
Several assessment measures were conducted at the end of the first experimental year. These included:

1. Evaluation by our Board of Advisors. Curriculum and pedagogy changes were submitted to our Board of Advisors, a group of executives who meet semi-annually to assist us with our programs. Board of Advisor feedback was over-whelmingly positive.

2. Exit Interview Feedback from Students. All graduating seniors were (and continue to be) interviewed and asked specific questions about classes and curriculum).

3. Comprehensive Content-Based Examination. One of our fears was that if we stressed process and the teaching of skills, content knowledge might decline. To assess whether or not there was a decrease in content knowledge, a comprehensive, content-based exam is given at the end of each year. The results indicate that students have not suffered any measurable loss of content knowledge. (And, although we don't teach to professional examinations, pass rates on CPA and other professional exams is as high as it has ever been.)

4. Analysis of Drop-Out Rate. It was our expectation that extensive use of groups would provide support for struggling students and that the student drop-out rate would decrease. In fact, the drop-out rate, which used to be 10-15 percent in intermediate accounting, is now less than two percent. (Part of the decrease may be due to the better quality students who are enrolling.)

5. <u>Course and Teacher Evaluations by Students.</u> Evaluations were mandated in every course by every instructor, both in core and non-core classes. Evaluations in the core were compared with those in other courses. No significant difference in teacher ratings was noted although course evaluation scores increased in the new curriculum.

6. <u>Student Surveys.</u> Comprehensive student surveys were conducted at the end of the year. Student feedback was extremely positive in favor of the changed curriculum.

7. <u>Faculty Surveys.</u> Comprehensive faculty surveys were conducted at the end of the year. Faculty feedback was also positive.

Summative Evaluation (Three and Four Years Later)

As of Fall, 1995, the new curriculum (although it was continuously being revised and improved) had been taught four times. As a result, we have been able to identify and use the following long-term measures:

1. <u>Number and Quality of Applicants to the Accounting Program.</u> We believed that if the changed program represented an improvement, both the quality and quantity of applicants would increase. During the past four years, the number of applicants to the undergraduate program has been 246 (1991), 284 (1992), 275 (1993), 304 (1994), and 352 (1995). The overall grade point averages of the classes have been 3.51, 3.56, 3.59, 3.58, and 3.62. We also calculate an algorithm based on introductory accounting class performance and several other measures. Average algorithms, where higher is better, for the past five years have been 1050, 1093, 1102, 1117, and 1127.

2. <u>Number and Quality of Student Placements.</u> We believed that if the quality of our program increased, recruiters would try harder to attract and hire our students. Every year the recruiting pressure for our students becomes more intense. "Big Six" hires of our students, for example, has increased from 59 in 1991 to approximately 150 in 1995.

3. <u>Recruiter Surveys.</u> During 1995, an extensive recruiter survey was conducted where those who hire at BYU were asked to compare our graduates with graduates of other top accounting programs. When skills and knowledge competencies were compared, our graduates ranked as "superior" in most cases and at least "equal to" in the others.

4. <u>Alumni Surveys.</u> During 1995, an extensive alumni survey was conducted where questions about quality of life, happiness with career, adequacy of career preparation, and BYU education were asked. This survey was part of an overall

university assessment effort. Accounting graduates from the past four years rated their educational experience and career satisfaction higher than any other major on campus.

5. Curriculum Awards. Our AECC project received the American Accounting Association's *Innovation in Accounting Education* award for outstanding curriculum innovation in 1994.

6. Rankings by Other Academics. During the past six years, BYU's *Public Accounting Report* ranking has increased from 13th at the undergraduate level and 8th at the graduate level to 3rd at both the graduate and undergraduate level.

7. Contributions from Alumni and Others. Although we didn't intend to use volume of gifts as an assessment measure, because of the increased interest in our program created by AECC changes, contributions to the SOAIS have increased dramatically. Two large gifts, one exceeding $2 million (some of it deferred) and one of approximately $300,000 were specifically made because of the donors' excitement for what we are doing.

Special Insights from Carrying Out Our AECC Grant

Faculty efforts in completing the AECC grant have made the entire faculty aware that lecture-based teaching, while efficient, is not very effective. We have recognized that students gain just as much knowledge from context-based, process-type learning as from spoon-feeding and required regurgitation. We have also discovered that using varied pedagogical approaches creates an excitement for teaching among faculty who previously had a tendency to get bored with continuous lecturing on the same topics. We have never had a greater effort from our faculty; yet, we have never had a happier faculty. We have also learned that students are capable of much more than we had given them credit. We are constantly amazed at what we can expect from students and how well students perform when given an opportunity. We have discovered that learning together with students is exciting.

Plans to Perpetuate the Changes That Worked Well

We have built the notion of continuous curriculum involvement into our strategic plan. We have organized our governance process into committees focusing on each of the goals in the strategic plan. We have a continuous improvement committee whose goal is to monitor curriculum and pedagogy and study ways to make improvements. This same group is also responsible for assuring that the successes of the junior core are translated into successes in beginning and advanced accounting classes. Our entire curriculum and pedagogy have changed because of our AECC project. We hold teaching improvement seminars on a regular basis with all faculty.

One of the distinguishing characteristics of our strategic plan is that we want to be known as "curriculum innovators." If anyone is going to leapfrog our curriculum, we want to be the school to do it.

Major Reports and Articles Generated from Grant Activities

"An Accounting Curriculum for the Next Century," *Issues in Accounting Education,* Vol. 9, No. 2, Fall 1994, W. Steve Albrecht, D. Cecil Clark, Jay M. Smith, Kevin D. Stocks, and Leon W. Woodfield, pp. 401-425.

"Emerging Competencies for the Practice of Accountancy," *Journal of Accounting Education,* Fall 1991, L.A. Deppe, E.O. Sonderegger, J.D. Stice, D.C. Clark, G.F. Streuling, pp. 257-290.

"An Analysis of the Use of Groups for Undergraduate and Graduate Accounting Students at Brigham Young University Between 1992 and 1994," J. Hardy and G.F. Streuling. (Has been submitted but not yet accepted.)

Materials Available to Send to Others and How to Get Them

Copies of the summary articles can be sent. In addition, our complete report or student workbooks can be made available for the cost of copying. Any other reasonable request will be honored.

Chapter 3
KANSAS STATE UNIVERSITY

Type, Size and Mission of Accounting Program

The mission of the Department of Accounting at Kansas State University (KSU) is to provide a balanced program of general, business, and accounting education at both the undergraduate and master levels which will prepare our students to become successful professional accountants, and to provide an intellectual climate which encourages and supports the offering of an accounting program of high academic quality.

Students apply to enter the accounting degree track after the completion of 60 credit hours and are accepted into the Department of Accounting with a 2.5 cumulative GPA. Students receive a Bachelor of Science (B.S.) degree after completing 126 approved credit hours and a Masters of Accountancy degree with the successful completion of an additional 30 approved credit hours.

Approximately 170 students graduate in accounting at the undergraduate level each year, with an additional 45 graduates from the Masters program. The Department of Accounting student body is primarily full-time traditional students from Kansas and the surrounding states.

Characteristics of Program Before the Grant

KSU Department of Accounting graduates were exposed to the technical concepts and procedures they needed to become successful accountants. The sequence of courses and topics were the same as in most traditional accounting programs. The sequence was driven by both pedagogical tradition and the nature of textbooks used. The approach frequently offered the student both a simple concept and a more complex concept (based on the simpler one) at virtually the same time. Given that the simple concept is the basis for understanding the more complex one, the approach forced students to memorize rather than think and understand. Lack of attention to sequencing also caused problems for students by providing them with more information than they could absorb, given that they lacked a meaningful cognitive structure within which to interpret new pieces of information. Faculty primarily used the lecture method. The group work method was not utilized and professional skills were not emphasized.

Central Objective of Grant

KSU's AECC project had three broad objectives.

I. **To provide accounting students with sufficient technical and professional knowledge to form the foundation for a successful accounting career.**

This objective focuses on developing accounting knowledge as a coherent whole. Students must understand that accounting is an information discipline. They must appreciate that this information discipline is based on the notions of capturing, controlling, and reporting information whether the intended report is a tax return or production report. We believe that our students were always exposed to the technical concepts and procedures they needed to become successful accountants. Our objective is to enhance our students' ability to understand and retain those concepts and procedures.

In the area of professional knowledge, our objective is to present students with a more complete view of the professional requirements they will face. This includes a greater familiarity with the professional literature and how to use this literature as guidance in resolving professional dilemmas. This area encompasses issues such as ethics and the challenge of integrating professional and personal lives. We also want to build a global perspective and encourage computer literacy as part of the curriculum.

II. **To provide accounting students with the skills necessary to implement their knowledge in the professional accounting environment.**

Implicit in this objective is development of these skills as part of the pedagogical approach in our accounting curriculum. These skills include the ability to:

*communicate effectively:
It is our objective to develop communication skills both in written and oral communications. We view communication as a dialogue. Thus, listening and understanding messages received are as important as sending clear, concise messages.

*analyze and resolve problems:
Our objective is to enhance our students' ability to deal with more complex, ambiguous fact situations. We employ a pedagogical approach where, in its later stages, students must identify problems, formulate and evaluate solutions, and choose and justify an alternative. This level of problem-solving is the end product of our curriculum and is developed throughout the educational process.

*deal effectively with other people:

Our objective is to help our students to understand the need for and benefits of interpersonal skills in their professional careers. Providing some formal training in areas such as team-building and negotiation, then having them practice specific skills in the context of group projects, assures that they know what interpersonal skills are and how those skills may be effectively employed.

*learn new ideas and techniques that are encountered after the students end their formal education:

The ability to accept and learn new concepts and techniques means that the students will be better able to deal with our rapidly changing world. This objective goes beyond merely adapting to technological changes. We provide courses that will help the student develop a perspective or "world view" that will accommodate new ideas and information.

III. To attract and retain students with the talents required for success in the accounting profession.

Our third objective is to attract and retain students who have characteristics that yield greater promise of success as professional accountants. Evidence has shown that the accounting profession has a negative stereotype among the very students who would be desirable candidates for the accounting profession. Given this evidence, revision of curriculum alone will not be sufficient to bring the best and brightest to the accounting profession. Developing a recruitment program to compliment the curriculum revision will improve the quality of student in our program and should improve the career awareness of the profession throughout the state and region.

Key Means of Accomplishing Grant Objective

The original grant proposal was developed by an eight-person committee made up of five members from the Accounting Department and three members from outside the College. Based on input from the entire accounting faculty, this committee developed the original model for the curriculum, suggested teaching methods that were appropriate to achieve our educational objectives, and developed a recruitment program. The committee's proposal was implemented by assigning individual faculty with responsibility for coordinating faculty efforts in three areas: curriculum and pedagogy development, student recruitment, and assessment. The department head served as the overall coordinator and worked very closely with area coordinators.

The grant proposed a new model for accounting education and resulted in a complete revision of our curriculum. Implementation required the replacement of the traditional curriculum with the new curriculum. Since current students were in various stages of completion under the traditional program and because we hoped to collect comparative assessment data, we chose to phase in the new program by offering both the new and the old curriculum concurrently during the transition. Students already in the traditional program or entering the program were given the choice of which curriculum they wanted to follow. This election was awarded only in the initial year of implementation. Thereafter, all entering students enrolled in the new curriculum. The curriculum was phased in over a five-year period beginning with the sophomore level introductory courses.

Major Changes from Pre-Grant Conditions

STUDENT RECRUITMENT: K-State is an open enrollment university. Prior to the grant, the Accounting Department did no active recruiting. We relied on university and department reputations to attract students. Because of budgetary limitations and growth in the university's student body, we had a problem of too many students in accounting. Under this scenario, it may seem odd to develop an aggressive program to recruit students. Our interest was not in attracting more students, but rather to attract high quality students with the characteristics needed for success in the accounting program.

KSU has developed a comprehensive recruiting program to attract the best and brightest students to the accounting profession. Recruiting is an important aspect of our program changes. Its inclusion is based on evidence of a negative stereotype of accounting and accountants and on a belief that quality students are necessary for our curriculum revision to be effective. Our student recruitment program is designed to accomplish two goals. The first is to make quality high school and college students aware of the challenges and opportunities in the accounting profession. The second is to promote KSU's revised accounting program. To accomplish these goals a three-part program has been developed.

The first part is designed to develop a network of high school teachers and counselors in our geographic region who have an accurate perception of the career opportunities in accounting. This part of the program strives to identify the high school teachers and counselors who are particularly influential in the career decisions of their students. We ask accounting students at KSU to identify the key teachers and counselors at their high schools. Once identified, these teachers and counselors are invited to a campus presentation on career opportunities in accounting and the accounting program at KSU. The impetus for the first part of our recruiting program is the notion that many high school teachers and counselors are as unaware of the challenges and opportunities in accounting as their students. Correcting these misperceptions increases the likelihood of students getting more accurate information about accountancy from their career advisors.

The second part is designed to identify and recruit high quality students to the accounting program. High school and undecided college students are invited to campus to hear our presentation on career opportunities in accounting. As with the teachers and counselors, the goal is to improve awareness of accountancy and to promote KSU's accounting program. A recruitment video has also been developed with resources provided by outside constituents. The video and related brochure are sent to all high school students identified as having an interest in an accounting career.

The third part of our recruitment effort is the establishment of an Accounting Advocates group selected from our student body. Their primary responsibility is to participate in our student recruitment program. They help organize the recruitment presentations, make presentations to high schools in the area, help in the identification of high school and undecided college students for recruitment, and work with alumni and friends of KSU's accounting program on recruitment. The Accounting Advocates will keep this designation upon graduation, and thus create a network of KSU alumni that can promote the accounting profession and the KSU accounting program.

CURRICULUM: Our AECC changes resulted in a comprehensive revision of our curriculum based on a logical sequence of courses and topics that emphasizes providing students with simple concepts prior to exposing them to more complex topics. Our curriculum is designed to provide students with a broad understanding of accounting as an information system in the sophomore and junior years and to build on this foundation by providing them with more complex and specialized issues in their senior and fifth year.

> INTRODUCTORY COURSES – Sophomore Year
> Courses: Accounting for Business Operations (3 credit hours)
> Accounting for Investing and Financing (3 credit hours)

The two introductory courses are developed from a user perspective. Students learn that the function of any accounting system is to provide information useful for economic decision-making. The material is separated based on the type of decision to be made. The courses emphasize:

- accounting's role in providing information to a variety of users: businesses, investors, government, and other stakeholders,
- the basic features of the recording and reporting of accounting information,
- the basic principles underlying the development and function of an effective accounting information system,
- the fundamental accounting concepts and principles, and
- the learning of accounting by using accounting information to make and evaluate economic decisions.

Through this course, students begin to understand what accounting and the accounting profession are about. They gain an appreciation for the personal and academic characteristics needed to be an accountant and the wide variety of career opportunities available.

> DEVELOPMENT OF AN ACCOUNTING FRAMEWORK – Junior Year
> Courses: Accounting Processes and Controls (4 credit hours)
> Accounting Theory and History (3 credit hours)

It is important for students to see the accounting environment as a system that must be capable of serving all users. Therefore, we introduce the accounting system as a framework that has evolved over time and in response to different and often changing needs. We achieve this through two courses that address the needs of all users.

Accounting Processes and Controls is a pivotal course in the curriculum. The premise of the course is that accounting students do not have extensive business experience and they do not understand the "micro-level" workings of businesses. Therefore, the emphasis is on understanding how information systems capture, summarize, and report useful, relevant information. Students learn that the accounting system is more than ledgers and journals; it is a necessary means of making sense of the complex, dynamic business environment.

The course is organized so that students understand the flow of information through an enterprise, the sources and nature of documents, and the controls necessary to insure the accuracy and reliability of information. It accomplishes two major purposes. First, student see the nature of the transactions that occur across the entire scope of business activities. Students deal with the decisions that initiate transactions, the timing of events associated with transactions, and the documents involved. This includes understanding both transaction cycles within the system and accounting cycles. Second, this course allows the students to develop the fundamental concepts and ideas that underlie many of the reporting and decision-making activities that are the focus of later courses.

The Accounting Theory and History course focuses on valuation and measurement issues. In order for accounting data to be informational it must be responsive to user needs. These needs have changed over time and differ with respect to the specific user and type of decision being made. Also, this course looks at the history of accounting and illustrates how it has evolved over time in response to the changing needs of users. It examines alternative valuation and measurement methods and discusses the strengths and weaknesses of these methods with respect to different types of decisions and users. Through this course, students broaden their understanding of accounting as a source of information and of the need for accounting to be sufficiently flexible to serve the information requirements of a variety of users.

> CORE COURSES – Last semester Junior Year and Senior Year
> Courses: Financial Reporting (3 credit hours)
> Managerial Reporting (3 credit hours)
> Taxation I (3 credit hours)
> Reporting for Not-for-Profit Entities (3 credit hours)
> Auditing (3 credit hours)

In the core, the coursework turns to the specific accounting needs of four user groups: external users (Financial Reporting), internal users (Managerial Reporting), government (Taxation), and users of not-for-profit entity information. The core also includes a traditional audit course.

The first three groups are the primary users to whom almost all profit-oriented entities must provide accounting information. Each group has unique information needs and places specific requirements on the company. The accounting system for most businesses must be designed to provide financial statements and other accounting information required of these user groups. Therefore, students must become knowledgeable with respect to the requirements of each group.

The fourth user group has unique information requirements, not as much the result of the specific user but rather the result of the unusual nature of the business entity. Not-for-profit entities are growing in number and importance. This group includes entities such as churches, school districts, and governmental organizations. Because these organizations have unique stewardship roles and are often constrained by legal restrictions, the accounting systems and information provided by these systems are unique.

To this point, the student has learned that accounting is a process of gathering economic/financial data and presenting it in a manner useful for decision making. However, the accounting profession has also accepted the responsibility for providing an independent verification of the financial statements presented to external users through the audit function. The auditing course content is the same as in most traditional accounting curriculums.

RESEARCH – Last Semester Senior Year
Course: Accounting Research (3 credit hours)

The final course taken at the undergraduate level is Accounting Research. This course focuses on self-learning skills and the ability to solve complex, ambiguous problems. In order to resolve these problems, students learn the sources of guidance for taxation problems (e.g., Tax Code, court cases, etc.) and other reporting issues (e.g., FASB Standards, Interpretations, etc.) and how to use them. The fact situations are in the form of cases. The students not only learn how to conduct professionally-oriented research, but they receive formal training on how to analyze and present cases. In addition, they receive formal training in how to write professional communications, such as memoranda.

AREAS OF SPECIALIZATION – Fifth Year
Specialization Tracks: Tax
Financial Reporting and Auditing
Managerial/Controllership

In the fifth year all students take a three-credit-hour Advance Financial Reporting class and four additional courses in their chosen area of specialization. These tracks allow students to focus on specific career objectives. These courses are the culmination of the student's formal education. The predominant pedagogical approach is case analysis, and employs the skills learned in the research course. Students are evaluated on written analysis and participation in class discussion.

Methods of Achieving Faculty and Administrative Support of the Changes Undertaken

Prior to submission of the grant proposal we obtained letters of administrative support from the President of the University, the Provost, and the Dean of the College. All three administrators are proponents of educational innovation and recognize the need for change.

The faculty are also supportive of change. They want to be active participants in the change process. Faculty support for changes was directly related to their opportunity to be a part of the change process. For this reason, it was essential for the curriculum coordinator to get all faculty involved in some aspect of the revision. Each faculty member was asked to be involved in the development of all courses in their area of specialization. Also, all faculty were asked to participate in the overall evaluation of all new courses through development and implementation. Though individual involvement varied, faculty were provided an opportunity to be active participants in the process. Thus all faculty could take ownership in the new curriculum.

Although it was essential for our change that all faculty accept the new model, it did not require them to give up their freedom to add their own touches to the courses. We all agreed on the content and educational objectives of each course; however, each faculty was given freedom in the teaching of the course. They were allowed to choose teaching methods that they found to be the most successful in achieving the course objectives.

Change Activities That Worked Well and Which Others Might Copy

The curriculum project resulted in a complete revision of our program. Such a sweeping change may be too aggressive for many schools. However, there are many aspects of our change that work well and which could easily be adopted by any program.

• Our introductory courses serve the entire campus. The majority of students in the course are nonaccounting majors. These courses were redesigned to focus on how accounting information is used in making business decisions. Redevelopment of the course to a user perspective helps the students understand the role of accounting information and better addresses the needs of both accounting and nonaccounting majors.

• The Theory and History course has worked well in developing our students' professional skills. The conceptual nature of the course is difficult for many students; however, the nontechnical, non-rule oriented material provides a unique environment to challenge the students' communication and critical thinking skills. Students are put into a situation in which they must evaluate both sides of numerous theoretical issues, recognize the needs of various user groups, and organize their thoughts into clear and concise presentations. Few traditional accounting courses provide this same type of opportunity. The course also reemphasizes the role of accounting information in decision making, how accounting responds to the changing and different needs of various user groups, and the importance of professional skills.

• All programs need to create an educational environment that prepares their graduates to function in a professional environment. This requires the student to be knowledgeable about the sources of professional authority, how to efficiently and effectively use these sources, and how to use and communicate this knowledge. The Accounting Research course has worked extremely well in developing these skills in our graduates. This course focuses on self-learning skills and uses the case method exclusively. Our students are asked to solve complex, ambiguous problems using available authoritative sources. Through the course, students learn how to conduct professionally-oriented research and how to analyze and present cases. Also, they receive formal training in how to write professional communications. Upon completion of the course, the students are very familiar with the sources available in a professional library and how to use them. Although this course is very demanding for both faculty and students, we believe such a course should be included in every accounting program.

• There is general agreement that accounting programs must provide their graduates with the professional skills necessary to be effective in their profession. We have chosen to accomplish this through a combination of curriculum and pedagogical changes. Many schools may find major curriculum change to be difficult or slow to accomplish. Nevertheless, changes in how courses are taught can result in immediate improvement in the professional skills of accounting graduates and can be implemented by any program, with or without curriculum revision. The traditional lecture method and objective tests are often effective approaches when the educational objective is to provide students with basic knowledge and comprehension of simple concepts. However, when the educational objective is for students to develop higher order cognitive skills necessary to solve complex problems, and to select among competing alternatives, the lecture method is ineffective. We have found the use of cooperative learning techniques and the case method to be necessary in developing students' professional skills. Also, we had to change how we assess student performance. Assessment needs to include the evaluation of class preparation and participation, tests with free-response questions, and the evaluation of written and oral presentations. These changes can be made at the individual faculty level and can be effectively implemented in any curriculum. These methods do require an increased time commitment and greater subjective evaluation by the faculty; however, they can be effectively used to develop and evaluate the skill-based competencies desired of students.

• Kansas State has developed a proactive recruitment program that educates high school and undecided college students about the nature of the accountant's work and accounting career opportunities. Our recruitment efforts have been on attracting students who possess the innate characteristics and skills that evidence promise of success as professional accountants. This effort has been supported entirely by external funding and has been effective in attracting high quality students to our program. It has also improved our reputation as a leader in accounting education in the state and region.

Change Activities Undertaken That Did Not Work

Our changes were phased in over several years. During the early period of the change the major emphasis was on our introductory courses, and two faculty had responsibility for their development. The development of these courses included the development of textbooks and other materials that emphasized the user perspective of accounting information. Although the courses were developed and implemented as planned, we learned two things from the process. First, through the development process the two faculty involved invested so much time and interest in the courses that they took a strong ownership interest in them. During this same period, the other faculty did not feel involved in the change process and lost some of the initial enthusiasm for what we were doing. In order to keep everyone involved, we established a review process for new course development that allowed all faculty to play a role in evaluating course developments based on our established course objectives. This process has helped to create faculty, rather than individual, ownership in our course and curriculum changes.

Second, through this process we recognized the tremendous time and faculty resource commitment needed for course material development, especially textbooks. Based on these early experiences we reduced the amount of new material developed in our other courses. Instead of using textbooks as the foundation for our new courses, we use them as a resource. Students are provided with a course outline that serves as the framework of the course, and they use several sources of information throughout the class period. These sources include professional authorities, textbooks, and developed materials. This reduces the amount of new materials that need to be developed and increases course flexibility since the textbook no longer drives the course. Although there was some early resistance by students accustomed to textbook driven courses, they quickly adapted to this approach.

Unexpected Benefits from Change Activities

Although we have a very dedicated faculty, the change created an unexpected enthusiasm and renewed commitment toward teaching responsibilities and our overall educational program. This attitude is contagious and has carried over to the entire College, which is now going through a similar change.

Another unexpected benefit has been the national interest and support of our change activities by business, the profession, and other accounting programs.

Measurement of the Effects of Changes Accomplished

As with all aspects of program development, assessment is a continuous process. The Department's assessment activities can be divided into two parts. First, as part of our original proposal we identified several assessment activities that we hoped to undertake. These activities have either been accomplished or have been delayed/ dropped because of resource limitations. Second, we have identified those activities that are most cost effective and which have become a part of our ongoing assessment program.

Original Proposed Assessment Activities

1.   As part of our assessment program, graduating seniors, one-year alumni, and four-year alumni are surveyed once every four years. Accounting majors were surveyed in 1989 and in 1993. In 1993, only the graduating seniors had completed the new program (or at least four years of it), so the alumni portion of the survey provides only baseline data until 1997.

2.   Institutional funds were to be used to develop a "capstone" test in the area of accounting. The exam was to be used to test students' abilities at all six levels of Bloom's taxonomy of cognitive objectives as well as the content areas included in the new curriculum. Test results for graduating seniors in 1991 and 1992 were to be compared to the results of seniors who complete the new curriculum. Because of legislative budget cuts to the university, we were informed that institutional funds were no longer available to develop the "capstone" test. This activity has been dropped.

3.   Students' writing was sampled at the end of their sophomore year and again near graduation. Statistically significant improvement in students' writing ability is expected. Graduating seniors completing the new curriculum were videotaped to assess their oral communication skills. A substantial percentage of all graduating students will be expected to demonstrate acceptable oral communications competency. However, old-versus-new comparisons will involve a certain amount of subjectivity since any "blind" evaluator would be able to differentiate the "setting" of the recorded presentations. An evaluation will be made by an expert outside of the college provided it is determined that the differences in the settings between old and new curriculum seniors will not invalidate the comparison.

4.   Examinations in each of the courses will be reviewed by experts (peers) to determine whether the exams match course objectives with regard to Bloom's taxonomy of cognitive objectives. For example, if a course is to stress application and analysis, it would be expected that the examinations, papers, etc. in that course will place the greatest emphasis on those abilities.

An individual from the College of Education was hired to make a seminar presentation to our faculty on what assessment techniques are appropriate for measuring the various levels of Bloom's taxonomy. Specific examples were presented.

For each course, faculty were required to identify by topic/subject matter at what level they wanted their students to learn and to identify the assessment techniques they would use to evaluate the students' performance. During the summer we identified the first three courses to be reviewed. During the 1995-96 academic year, the assessment activities of these courses were examined to ensure that they match the course objectives. The other courses will be similarly evaluated over the following two years.

5. In Spring 1992, we administered the American College Testing (ACT) Program's new critical thinking test and their College Student Outcomes Survey to over 300 students in our second accounting class (Accounting for Investing and Financing). The results indicate that our students scored above the national average.

6. We administered the Ennis-Weir test of critical thinking to four-year graduates of the old and new curricula in the Spring of 1993. Dr. Don Hatcher from Baker University was brought in to describe his experiences in administering the exam to over 1,000 students at his school and to conduct a training session for our faculty (who had previously agreed to grade the essay-type exam). Student responses were typed and identified only by number by department secretarial staff. They were then graded on a double-blind basis (i.e., each student's paper was graded by two different faculty). New curriculum students scored statistically significantly higher. However, the students were not randomly placed into the two different curricula.

Ongoing Assessment Program

In 1995 we developed an exit interview instrument for graduating seniors. The interview instrument is used to collect a variety of information on our program. It is currently being revised because some items were structured such that it was difficult to interpret student responses. In addition to assessments based on student responses, the Department surveys interviewers and employers of our graduates. These surveys focus on the technical and professional skills of our graduates and how they compare to graduates of other programs.

The Department is also working with the University's Office of Educational Advancement to develop a program to evaluate senior and graduate students' critical thinking level. This program, based on student interviews, began in the Spring 1996 semester.

It will be several years before we will be able to fully assess the impact of our changes. Nevertheless, current results suggest that our students compare favorably with other programs and placement of our graduates is strong. Based on our University placement center data, we have ninety to ninety-five percent placement of our graduates in either accounting-related positions or graduate education. We also know current graduates believe the accounting program does a better job of addressing professional skill development than alumni graduating under the old curriculum.

Special Insights from Carrying Out Our AECC Grant

Accounting programs are under a lot of pressure to change. We are being told that our graduates are not prepared to work in a rapidly changing profession. We are told that we are not attracting the best and brightest students. We are being told that we are not devoting enough time or attention to teaching and too much time researching esoteric issues.

The typical criticism of accounting education is founded in truth but almost always exaggerated. This has two effects. One, they are easily dismissed as over-statements by those not wanting change. Two, they are often interpreted as indicating the need for a major overhaul by those supporting change. It seems to us that exaggerating the problem is very divisive. It tends to separate faculty rather than bring them together with a common goal.

The academic environment is one based on tradition. It holds tightly to the time honored independence of faculty with respect to their classes and their scholarship. Our evaluation and reward system is based on individual efforts, and the most respected attribute of our faculty is an independence of thought. Under this environment our academic programs were and continue to be recognized as the finest in the world, and we can all point to a long list of successful business leaders who were a product of this system. With this in mind, no one should be surprised to find resistance to change.

The key to successful educational change is faculty ownership. You can not force change on faculty; they must buy into it. Faculty have differing views about change. Some believe the current system is working fine for them, while others desire to change the entire system. The key to success will be the ability of the faculty to respect differing points of view.

Change is not an all or nothing situation. It can take place at any level. It does not require the commitment and agreement on the part of the entire faculty. It does not require a complete curriculum revision to be meaningful. Individuals wishing to try new approaches should be encouraged to do so, while at the same time respecting the views of faculty who are cautious or resistant toward new developments.

Change often takes place in small steps. It is high risk and requires a long-range commitment by the involved faculty. Change is time consuming and requires considerable faculty development. It is essential that the faculty evaluation system be structured to both encourage and reward faculty committed to educational improvement. This requires administrative support.

Not all changes are good. Many attempts are not successful. It is very important that change be tied to educational objectives. Faculty must make careful periodic assessments of the effect of new approaches on accomplishing these objectives. Ineffective changes need to be revised or abandoned.

Plans to Perpetuate the Changes That Worked Well

It is our belief that change is a continuous process. Implementation of our new curriculum is not the end but the beginning of the change process. Our curriculum changes have been fully implemented since the Spring 1995 semester. The faculty believe that the new educational model is achieving the educational objectives of the program. We continue to review and improve the curriculum and teaching methods being used based on new information being collected.

Major Reports and Articles Generated from AECC Grant Activities

Ainsworth, Penne, Dan Deines, David Plumlee and Cathy Larson, *Introduction to Accounting: A Planning, Performing, and Evaluating Approach* (Homewood, Illinois; Richard D. Irwin), 1995.

Ainsworth, P., *"Restructuring the Introductory Accounting Courses: The KSU Experience,"* Journal of Accounting Education, 1995.

Ainsworth, P. and R. David Plumlee, *"Restructuring the Accounting Curriculum Content Sequence; The KSU Experience,"* Issues in Accounting Education, Spring 1993.

Ainsworth, P., *"Flint Hills Salon: A Case Analysis"* (New York; John Wiley and Sons), 1992.

Materials Available to Send to Others and How to Get Them

The Kansas State Accounting Department is preparing a monograph that will provide more detailed information about our Project and the courses that make up our new curriculum. This monograph will be made available for a small fee to cover the cost of copying and mailing. Persons interested in obtaining a copy should contact:

Department of Accounting
Calvin Hall 109A
Kansas State University
Manhattan, KS 66506
913-532-6184

Chapter 4
KIRKWOOD COMMUNITY COLLEGE

Type, Size and Mission of Accounting Program

The accounting program at Kirkwood Community College provides instruction in several areas. First, there is a two-year program in which the students intend to enter the job market at the completion of the program and obtain entry level accounting positions (Accounting Associates). In addition to the introductory accounting courses, these students take two semesters of intermediate accounting, one semester of cost accounting, one semester of income tax, and one semester of computer applications in accounting.

Second, the program offers the first two years of a four-year degree program. The students in this track enroll with the expectation of transferring to a four-year college and obtaining degrees. Most of these students taking accounting courses are Business Administration majors. In general, these students will not take accounting courses beyond the introductory course at Kirkwood Community College. Third, other two-year degree programs, such as computer programming, which require one or two semesters of beginning accounting, are offered.

Finally, as the result of the Accounting Education Change Commission grant, Kirkwood now offers two introductory accounting courses, each two semesters in length and four (4) hours of credit for each semester. These two courses are the traditional preparers course, titled Principles of Accounting, and a new course emphasizing understanding financial statements and titled Introduction to Accounting. Both of these courses are accepted for transfer credit. In each course, the student must receive credit for both semesters in order to receive transfer credit for accounting at the state universities. A student who starts in one of the introductory courses cannot effectively transfer to the other introductory course at the end of the first semester, since the two courses do not cover the content material in the same order.

Approximately 1,200 students enroll in the introductory accounting course each year. The number of students who take the introductory course typically is split about equally between full-time and part-time students. Statistics are not available for the distribution of traditional vs. non-traditional students enrolled in the accounting courses, but observation would indicate that approximately 70-80% of the daytime students is traditional and 20-30% of the evening students is traditional. The Principles of Accounting and the Introduction to Accounting courses have no prerequisites. The majority of students enrolling in these courses are first-year students.

Characteristics of Program Before AECC Grant

Prior to receiving the AECC grant, all accounting courses were taught using traditional methods and content. Introductory accounting sections were open to all students, regardless of major or program. The course was designed such that no differentiation was made for the differing needs of students enrolled in different programs. Five full-time faculty and 10-15 part-time faculty taught all of the accounting courses.

Central Objectives of AECC Grant

The AECC grant addressed only the first course in accounting. Our objectives are listed and explained in this section.

A. Change the introductory accounting course from the traditional preparers' perspective to a user perspective

One element of this objective was to reduce the time spent in the course on the basic bookkeeping elements of accounting. The impact of transactions on the financial statements would become the focal point of discussion, rather than the processes of recording the transactions. A second element of this objective is to incorporate decision-making aspects of accounting into the course. One method of accomplishing this is by intermingling managerial topics with financial topics.

B. Encourage good students to become professional accountants

Experience indicates that many students expressing interest in becoming accountants are actually interested in bookkeeping. They enjoy the recording aspects of accounting and do well in the bookkeeping phase of the course. However, many of these students have no interest and/or skills in the analytical aspects of accounting. Good students with problem-solving skills find the typical accounting courses are unchallenging and boring and decide that accounting is not interesting enough to attract them into the profession.

C. Improve students' communication skills

A primary objective is to incorporate writing as one of the major components of the course. More written assignments will be required for evaluation purposes, tests will include more essay and short answer items, and students will be required to co-enroll in a technical writing course geared to business writing. Also, students will be required to make more short presentations in the class.

D. Develop critical thinking skills

More problems that involve decision-making will be required. Also, we will attempt to make students more aware of their own thinking processes and help them improve these processes. In addition, students will be required to co-enroll in a critical thinking course.

E. Develop students' knowledge of the environment in which businesses operate

Materials will be developed to increase the students' understanding of the nature of business activities before discussing the accounting for the activities. Also, we will focus on the interrelationship of accounting with society.

F. Make the course more "real-world"

Current newspaper and magazine articles will be used as the basis for discussion of accounting topics. Corporate annual reports, 10-K's and proxy statements will be used for analysis. In addition, we will incorporate the use of computers into the course.

G. Serve the needs of non-accounting majors

For non-accounting majors, the goal is to develop knowledge related to the use of financial statements for personal use (e.g., for investment decision-making), as well as management decision-making in a business. The content will be changed to materials that the student may be more likely to remember five years after the course is completed.

H. Improve students' ability to work in groups

To enhance team skills of students, cooperative learning will be employed in the classroom.

I. Vary teaching methodologies

The focus in the classroom will be on learning rather than teaching. As a result, a variety of teaching methodologies will be employed to achieve various learning objectives and to match the learning styles of different types of learners.

J. Ensure that the course would be accepted for transfer credit

Means of Accomplishing Grant Objectives

Two faculty members were assigned for one year to course development. One faculty member had full-time release from teaching and one faculty member had three-fourths release time from teaching. During the course development, the developers performed the following activities:

A. Reviewed the curriculum changes being undertaken by other institutions, particularly recipients of other AECC grants.

B. Created an advisory committee to assist in selection of course topics. This committee consisted of representatives from local employers of graduates, faculty members from other disciplines at Kirkwood Community College, and accounting faculty from public and private universities to which Kirkwood Community College students typically transfer.

C. Reviewed the content of the major Accounting Principles texts to identify topics typically included and excluded from traditional courses.

D. Researched materials in other disciplines that were addressing some of the same concerns expressed by accounting educators.

E. Researched a wide variety of materials related to critical thinking and learning to learn.

F. Developed a working outline for the new course, eliminating many traditional topics and incorporating new topics.

Major Changes from Pre-Grant Conditions

As a result of the grant activities, an introductory accounting course entitled Introduction to Accounting, which emphasizes the use of accounting information, is available to all students. The Introduction to Accounting course is the recommended course for non-accounting business majors.

Methods of Achieving Faculty and Administrative Support for Changes

Prior to applying for the grant, the faculty of Kirkwood's accounting department had meetings regarding the changes to be made in the course. During these meetings, some members of the faculty expressed concern over the changes to be made and preferred that the department not apply for the grant. The dean of the business department (a CPA who previously taught accounting at Kirkwood Community

College) was a driving force in recruiting the faculty members who supported the grant to write the grant proposal. The dean indicated full support for the project and the proposed changes. The actual grant proposal was supported and signed by the President of Kirkwood Community College.

During the course development phase, the faculty members designing the course met regularly with the other faculty to discuss the specifics of the course changes. They also maintained contact with the schools accepting transfer credit so that Kirkwood Community College faculty and administrators could receive ongoing feedback that the new course was a viable alternative to the traditional approach. In addition, visits to our campus by AECC representatives helped to keep a high profile to our ongoing course development.

Change Activities Undertaken That Worked Well and Which Others Might Copy

The course development process discussed previously worked very well. In hindsight, we would not change the process in any major way. Most of the change activities may be described generally as either accounting content related or non-accounting content related.

Regarding accounting content related improvements, the change in emphasis has, in general, created more student interest in accounting as a topic for study. Students seem to develop a better knowledge of accounting as a result of the user orientation and other changes. Also, the increased interest has resulted in better student participation in class and other assignments. Development of students' knowledge of the business environment and of activities which result in recordable transactions has enhanced the students' understanding of accounting.

The new course serves well the needs of both accounting and non-accounting majors. Non-accounting majors will retain concepts for a longer period of time than they will retain procedures. Accounting majors will benefit from obtaining a way of thinking about accounting concepts before learning accounting procedures.

A number of students enrolled in the new course have indicated they were changing majors based upon the course. Feedback has been received from a relatively limited number of students at this point and may be similar to results in the traditional course. This information has been obtained in informal discussions with students and similar information may or may not be available from traditional courses. Five students who were changing to accounting indicated the reason for switching majors was a favorable attitude change about the nature of accounting work. The two students who changed from an accounting major switched because they did not previously recognize that accounting involved more than recording entries.

With regard to non-accounting content related improvements, students' communication skills have improved. The course requires much more writing and speaking than does the traditional course. Although we do not have any specific measurement instruments, it is obvious to us that the students' communications skills are improving as they progress through the course. The classroom environment is less formal than in a traditional lecture approach and the students interact more before and during class in the new classes as compared to the traditional classes. Also, critical thinking abilities improve during the course. The activities in which the students participate and the outside assignments required have been designed to promote critical thinking. As new topics are introduced, students are encouraged to make the connections with previous topics and classroom discussions often center around these student-discovered connections.

The students' ability to work in groups has been enhanced. Observation indicates that all students improve in this area. However, not all students achieve a high level ability in this area. Effective exchanges of course-related ideas emerge from the groups on a regular basis.

Varying the teaching methodologies to enhance students' learning has been a very educational and difficult process for us. We have been traditional lecturers for a long period of time and not necessarily very effective, at the beginning, in using new techniques. We believe we have become much better at the new methods and that the students are now benefiting from our improvement. Student reaction to a varied format has been very encouraging from both interest and learning perspectives.

Change Activities Undertaken That Did Not Work Well

The course is not as portable to other users as originally intended. There has been a lack of published materials available for many of the topics being covered. As a result, we have developed much of the material internally. At this point many of the materials are not supported by "how to" and "why" support materials. An outside user might have difficulty using some of the material without background information related to the purpose of the material and how to use it. This is a temporary situation and the necessary background material is being developed for future use.

Many faculty members at Kirkwood chose not to be involved in the change process and in the new course. This lack of widespread faculty involvement significantly limits the ability to expand this course offering.

As stated previously, the original grant proposal incorporated a requirement for students enrolling in the Introduction to Accounting I course to co-enroll in a critical thinking course taught by our English department faculty. This has been dropped as a requirement due to administrative concerns about part-time students and other restrictions that might limit enrollment. This requirement was in place for the first two years the course was offered and seemed to work well. We would encourage other institutions changing curricula to consider this as a requirement.

In a similar fashion, the original grant proposal incorporated a requirement for students enrolling in the Introduction to Accounting II course to co-enroll in a technical writing course taught by our English department faculty. This has been dropped as a requirement due to administrative concerns about part-time students and other restrictions that might limit enrollment. This requirement was in place for the first two years the course was offered and worked very well. Students were able to write about accounting and business related topics within both courses. We saw great improvement in the ability of the students to write effectively. We would encourage other institutions changing curricula as we have to consider this as a requirement.

Unexpected Benefits from Change Activities

Perhaps the greatest unexpected benefit from the change activities was meeting many dedicated accounting educators from around the country who are interested in improving the quality of accounting education. There is considerable interest in change and it has been extremely helpful to us to get insight from others as to the changes they are incorporating.

The change process rekindled interest in teaching for the change agents. One of the main reasons we applied for the grant was our belief that what we were teaching was not what the students needed. Discussing with students such topics as EDI, FASB activities, and why General Mill's earnings statement has a discontinued operations section is refreshing to us as instructors.

Our observations of student performance have been greatly expanded. In the traditional lecture method, the feedback as to student performance has been limited to evaluating test results. Working with students in small groups on a daily basis provides immediate feedback as to their areas of strengths and weaknesses.

We have broadened our assessment of the effect of the teaching methods we are using. Again, compared to the traditional lecture method, we are constantly trying new and different techniques when one method doesn't seem to work well. We have found that an approach that was successful for one topic and/or learning objective may not be successful for another topic and/or learning objective. In the lecture approach, it is easy to take great comfort in the fact that you got up in front of the class, told them what they need to know and if they don't get it, it is the students' fault. That attitude disappears when using other methods of instruction.

Measurement of the Effects of Changes Accomplished

To date, we have done no formal assessment of the effect of the changes. Any determination of improvements indicated previously is strictly from observation and is anecdotal. As discussed above, however, the observations are constant and ongoing.

Special Insights Gained from Carrying Out AECC Grant

There are many accounting educators who are interested in improving accounting education. However, relatively few of these educators are actually willing to undertake the difficult task of changing. Many of these faculty members seem to hope that major changes won't be necessary before they retire. Many accounting faculty seem perfectly willing to teach students the same topics they learned about accounting 20-30 years ago since that is what they know. Educators committed to change are often fighting an uphill battle, but they know they will be rewarded because their students will be receiving a better education than they would if they didn't make the effort.

The changes that are occurring cover a wide range of alternative models. The one-size-fits-all method of the past is gone. The changes that are occurring in business and technology will require a constant updating of the new courses. For example, when we started development of this course, the Internet was virtually unknown and Kirkwood Community College did not have access. We now have access to the Internet and one of the components of the new course now has students accessing Internet sites for information. In one module of the course, the students access the SEC files to obtain registration statements for both IPOs and seasoned offerings. The students use the information to determine the change in percentage ownership of the old stockholders and the effect on earnings per share. This helps the students to understand the effect of leverage much better than textbook illustrations of the topic.

Plans to Perpetuate the Changes That Worked Well

Kirkwood Community College has not put into effect any plan to perpetuate the changes. The current plan is to continue to have the same two instructors who developed the course teach it. We are not aware of any plans to have other instructors become involved in this course.

Major Reports and Articles Generated from AECC Grant Activities

While we have not written any reports, we have made presentations at more than 15 meetings and conferences around the country related to our course.

Materials Available to Others and How to Get Them

As discussed previously, the materials that we have developed may not be particularly useful without some background regarding how they are used. We are more than willing to share what we have. Requests for materials should be sent to Jack Zeller, Kirkwood Community College, 346LH, 6301 Kirkwood Blvd., Cedar Rapids, Iowa 52406. Also, Kirkwood Community College is in the process of developing a home page on the Internet and information on the project will ultimately be available through the Internet.

Chapter 5
MESA COMMUNITY COLLEGE
Introductory Accounting Courses: A User's Approach

Type, Size and Mission of Accounting Program

The mission of the accounting program at Mesa Community College (MCC) is to provide opportunities for lifelong learning to a diverse student population, promote excellence in teaching, learning and service, and encourage collaboration among students, faculty, staff and community, within a multicultural world.

In order to accomplish its mission, the MCC accounting program has three major objectives. First, coursework is offered which can be transferred to colleges and universities. Second, coursework is offered which can be applied to Associate of Applied Science (AAS) degrees and certificate programs. Third, coursework is provided for retraining and upgrading of skills to meet community needs. Admission to MCC requires that the student meet one of four criteria: (1) be a graduate of an accredited high school, (2) have a high school certificate of equivalency, (3) be 18 years of age or older and demonstrate evidence of potential success in the community college, or (4) be a transfer student in good standing from another college or university.

Business enrollments overall have been decreasing significantly over the past five years. Currently, there are 2,058 students enrolled in the College of Business at Arizona State University (ASU) who transferred from MCC. Approximately 400 of these students transferred in the past year. In the 1993-1994 academic year, 338 AAS degrees — 12 of which were accounting degrees — and one certificate in accounting were awarded. For the 1991-1992 academic year, which was prior to the receipt of the AECC grant, MCC served approximately 1,922 students in the traditional accounting sequence. Both the traditional accounting sequence and the new accounting courses developed under the AECC grant are currently being offered with 923 students being served in the 1994-1995 academic year. Of that amount, 338 students are enrolled in the new accounting sequence. MCC has a diverse student body, including in-state, out-of-state, and international students.

Characteristics of Program Before the Grant

The accounting program at MCC has been respected by both the community and ASU, the main recipient of MCC transfer students. However, before the AECC even came into existence, accounting faculty at MCC recognized that problems existed in the accounting courses offered. Of grave concern was the attrition rate in the first semester principles course. Approximately 50 percent of students withdrew from this course. Later documentation verified that MCC accounting courses had the highest attrition rate on campus, even higher than MCC math courses, which had been perceived as the courses with the worst attrition. Most of the accounting faculty at MCC felt that a key reason for the high withdrawal rate in their courses could be attributed to the poor basic skills of students enrolled. Attempts to require basic skills prerequisites for the first semester accounting principles course failed.

The actual content and delivery of accounting courses, combined with the attrition problem, had also discouraged some faculty from teaching the principles of accounting courses. One faculty member even switched into the statistics area on a full-time basis rather than teach accounting principles. Another faculty member began experimenting with group projects and other new teaching techniques to minimize the attrition problem as well as the drudgery of teaching accounting principles.

The introductory accounting sequence at MCC consisted of three three-credit courses, which transferred as six credits to most colleges and universities. The original intent of expanding to a nine-credit sequence was to offer a more in-depth, quality approach without having to rush through the material. As with most traditional introductory accounting courses, the focus of the course was a preparer's approach. Bookkeeping became the emphasis, the "one right answer" syndrome existed, and delivery was generally accomplished by the lecture method. The textbook, not the teacher, drove the course. Since many enrolled students lacked basic skills, learning mechanics such as debits, credits, and journal entries became a stumbling block. Faculty never had the time to allow students the chance to thoroughly learn and understand the theory behind what was being presented or even the purpose of the accounting information. Writing and oral communication skills, as well as team skills, were not a part of this sequence.

Central Objective of Grant

The main objective of MCC's AECC grant was to make substantial changes to the accounting curriculum which directly affected transfer students to the College of Business at ASU. A secondary objective was to apply the relevant portions of the new curriculum to the two-year degree and certificate programs.

To accomplish the main objective, it was decided that the new introductory accounting courses must include more than just technical accounting content. The accounting faculty decided the overriding goal of the redesigned curriculum should be to help develop in students the ability and motivation for life-long learning. The introductory accounting courses would be designed to meet the skill competencies necessary to transfer to the College of Business program at ASU and also to change from a knowledge-based emphasis to a process-oriented emphasis. Three significant changes would help accomplish the objectives of the AECC grant: (1) change the focus from the preparer's perspective to that of a user, (2) replace the lecture method with a variety of pedagogical techniques including cooperative learning, and (3) incorporate new skills such as writing, listening, speaking, team work, and critical thinking.

Key Means of Accomplishing Grant Objective

Prior to the receipt of the AECC grant, the six accounting faculty at MCC agreed that it was important to work closely with ASU on curriculum changes affecting the introductory accounting courses for transfer students. Two faculty members volunteered to meet on a regular basis with ASU accounting faculty to develop the new introductory sequence. Two other faculty members began working with ASU faculty on the development of the one-credit computer course which would also be required of accounting majors at ASU.

Meetings between MCC and ASU faculty occurred regularly for one semester. During this time a vision of the new courses was established and overall objectives were outlined. At this point, two significant events occurred: the AECC grant was awarded to MCC and the MCC faculty realized that curriculum development had to move at a quicker pace at the community college than at the university. Due to a much different bureaucratic process in the community college district, detailed course outlines and competencies needed to be submitted to ensure the new courses would be approved by the Governing Board. ASU faculty are not required to submit similar documents and therefore were able to take a slower, more methodical approach to the development of the courses. Both ASU and MCC faculty were confident that even though detailed lesson plans would be developed independently, the overall objectives would be met at both schools.

Reassigned time was given to three faculty to develop the new courses. This time was supported by the AECC grant. No other faculty received reassigned time.

The two MCC faculty who developed the new sequence of courses also taught the sequence for the first two years the courses were offered. A third faculty member, who had chosen to teach in the statistics area, decided to begin teaching accounting again in the third year of the new program. The faculty member who had developed a one-credit computer lab retired from the department and another faculty member took over this course. This faculty member also began teaching the new introductory courses in the fourth year of the program. In the third year of the new program, adjunct faculty were also hired to teach the new accounting courses in the evening program.

Major Changes from Pre-Grant Conditions

The traditional accounting sequence at MCC is composed of three three-credit courses, ACC111, ACC112, and ACC212. The first two courses focus on financial accounting topics and the third course focuses on managerial accounting. This nine-credit sequence is equivalent to the typical six-credit sequence taught at most colleges and universities. The textbook drives the course and competencies for the course mirror principles of accounting textbooks. Although the sequence continues to be taught, enrollment has dropped substantially due to the offering of the new accounting sequence.

The new sequence of courses is composed of two three-credit courses — ACC230 and ACC240 — and a one-credit, open-entry, open-exit, computer lab course — ACC250. Currently ACC250 is only required for non-ASU business transfer students and ASU accounting majors. The ACC230 and ACC240 courses are appropriately titled "Uses of Accounting Information I and II." The focus of these two courses is on how to use accounting information, not on how to prepare accounting reports. The ACC250 course, "Introductory Accounting Lab," covers the procedural details of bookkeeping and the preparation of financial accounting reports.

The new sequence of courses is unlike the traditional sequence in most respects. Some of the major changes to the courses include the following:

1. Prerequisites of critical reading, English, and college algebra have been added to the new sequence to ensure that students possess basic skills necessary to succeed.

2. Students do not learn bookkeeping concepts such as debits, credits, journal entries, posting to ledgers, or preparing financial statements; however, students do learn the concepts of bookkeeping through transaction analysis. The accounting equation is used throughout the courses to illustrate the effects of transactions on the financial statements.

3. Although the lecture method is sometimes used, the majority of class time includes cooperative learning activities and class discussion, which requires active participation of all students in the class.

4. The first five weeks of the ACC230 course are used for preliminary discussions including effective writing skills, decision making, forms of business organization, history and uses of accounting information, role of accounting organizations, transaction analysis, and the accrual versus the cash basis of accounting.

5. To teach accounting concepts, it was decided that a corporate annual report would be the basis for the course content. Students learn about accounting by walking through an entire annual report. The last ten weeks of the ACC230 course are spent on this task.

6. The first five weeks of the ACC240 course bring together what students learned in ACC230 through financial statement analysis. This serves as a good review of ACC230, while also teaching students techniques of a thorough analysis.

7. The second five weeks of ACC240 are used to discuss how internal accounting reports are used in a firm for decision making. Many topics are introduced just as they were in the traditional sequence; however, the emphasis is on comparing the traditional approach to more innovative approaches as outlined in business and accounting periodicals.

8. The last five weeks of ACC240 include a discussion of taxes and accounting issues in government. Oral presentations of student course projects are also given at this time.

9. The culmination of the new sequence is a course project which requires each student to analyze a company, write a report, and orally present the results of the analysis to the class.

10. Throughout the entire sequence students are required to turn in a variety of writing assignments, present material orally to the class, and work in teams.

Methods of Achieving Faculty and Administrative Support for Changes

The six accounting faculty at MCC unanimously voted to apply for the AECC grant. Two faculty members volunteered to develop and teach the new courses. Although all faculty were willing to support the efforts of these two faculty, it was clear that not all faculty wanted to be part of the development process.

The administration was at first reluctant to support the accounting project. However, once they realized that this change was necessary to continue a positive relationship with ASU, the necessary support was offered. The success of the new curriculum has convinced the administration that their final decision was the correct one. The Dean of Instruction was responsible for nominating the two faculty who developed the new courses for the "Innovator of the Year" award given annually.

Change Activities That Worked Well and Which Others Might Copy

The change activities which took place at MCC have been for the most part successful. Any of the changes implemented could be individually or collectively used at other colleges and universities. A brief description of successful change activities follows:

1. **Integration of nonaccounting skills into the curriculum**
    Based on recommendations by local employers, AECC position statements, and national surveys, the accounting faculty focused on integrating the following eight skills into the accounting courses:

    a. Written communication
    b. Oral communication
    c. Listening
    d. Critical reading
    e. Research
    f. Team work
    g. Analytical and critical thinking
    h. Time management

Incorporation of these skills has caused a significant change in grading procedures. Accuracy of technical accounting content is only a portion of the grade on each assignment. Points are also allocated for skill-based competencies. Examples of how the above skills have been included in the new accounting courses follow.

Team Work

Students work in teams during almost every class period. This offers students a chance to apply material that has been discussed in class or assigned for homework. While some of these assignments are quantitative, many are subjective in nature and require the application of the decision making process. Some assignments involve finding information in the financial statements and interpreting that information. The material is often processed as a class after teams have worked on the assignment.

The faculty have discovered that students like working in teams. Students are pleasantly surprised at the insights other students can bring to problems. They also feel comfortable voicing their opinions within the comfort zone of a group of people they know. However, problems with team work have occurred. Faculty have learned that team work results in positive experiences under the following circumstances:

1.   Careful attention is paid to the composition of the group. They should be heterogeneous based on ability, gender, and culture. Friends should be split up.

2.   Attendance policies must be enforced.

3.   Teams should be changed once or twice during a semester. Changing team members is often initially resisted by group members that have found a comfort zone, but welcomed after the change is made. By mid-semester there is much cross-pollination of ideas among groups because more students know each other.

4.   Group grades are rarely given for assignments. It is difficult to determine contributions of individual members.

Research Reports
Students are required to research an accounting topic. A written and oral report may be required. This assignment is graded for accuracy and quality of content, as well as for writing, speaking, and research skills. Listening, critical reading, and time management skills are also a part of this assignment. If the student does not follow the guidelines given by the instructor, or cannot read and understand information found at the library, his or her grade will be negatively affected. Since the daily class assignments continue regardless of due dates of individual reports, students must discipline themselves to complete this assignment as well as the daily assignments in a timely manner.

Mini-cases
Short cases are used to begin to develop students' critical thinking and analytical skills. These are unstructured problems which often do not have one right answer. Students must do a written analysis and defend their answers. Students find these time consuming, sometimes frustrating, but nearly always an exceptional learning tool.

Reading Logs
Because there is no one textbook which fits the needs of the new accounting courses, several textbooks are used, as well as periodical articles. Students answer questions on a reading log for all reading assignments from textbooks and periodicals. These logs are sometimes used as a basis for group discussion. Since students write peer evaluations of their team members, there is much peer pressure to come to class prepared with the reading log complete. These assignments help students develop critical reading and team skills.

2.   **Requiring prerequisites of critical reading, English, and college algebra**
     The changes discussed above would not have been successful at MCC if prerequisites had not been required. This change is particularly relevant to community colleges, while it may not be relevant to universities with high admission standards.

3.   **Switching from a preparer to a user approach in combination with a one-credit computer lab**
     A concern of accounting faculty was that students would not be able to change their mind and transfer to a four-year college other than ASU without losing accounting credits. As evidenced by positive articulation agreements with the two other major state universities — University of Arizona and Northern Arizona University — the combination of ACC230, ACC240, and ACC250 does

prepare business transfer students for most universities even if the transfer university has not made major accounting curriculum changes.

4. **Using an annual report as the driver of the course instead of a textbook**
   All faculty teaching the new accounting sequence are encouraged to use real annual reports in class. It has been fairly easy to obtain enough of the same company's reports by calling and requesting them from the corporate headquarters. An alternative source is to have students use the *Wall Street Journal* service to obtain a particular company's annual report.

Change Activities Undertaken That Did Not Work

The AECC grant allowed MCC to make significant and positive changes to the accounting curriculum; however, some proposed changes were not implemented or did not work. The main concerns and challenges faced by the accounting faculty are discussed below.

1. Change requires an enormous amount of time and dedication. As they currently exist, community colleges can be detrimental to change efforts. With over 20,000 students, MCC is a large campus. Smaller campuses are most likely in an even less envious position. Despite the size of MCC, only two faculty dedicated themselves to the AECC grant. One of these two faculty has now moved on to a new and unrelated change project. While accounting faculty at universities tend to be discipline specific, faculty at community colleges, including MCC, must often be certified to teach in more than one discipline. Faculty time is divided between two or more key efforts. Teaching loads average 15 credits per semester. Administrators consider most change efforts to be part of the faculty's normal duties and are, therefore, reluctant to support change efforts financially. For the accounting change to continue to be a success, it is important for administrators to recognize the time element required of all full-time and part-time faculty teaching the new accounting courses.

2. Although the prerequisites added to the accounting courses are perceived as successful, a change to those prerequisites occurred which has been viewed negatively by faculty in support of the AECC change. MCC is one of ten campuses in the Maricopa County Community College District. As a result, curriculum changes must be approved by all ten campuses. Significant resistance to the accounting change existed when the new accounting courses were approved. As a compromise, faculty developing the new courses agreed to allow an alternative prerequisite of ACC111. This prerequisite is contrary to the goals of the AECC grant. By taking the ACC111 course, which has not changed in content or pedagogy, students can enter the new accounting courses still lacking in basic skills.

3. Demand for the new accounting courses in the evening program has exceeded the supply of part-time faculty qualified to teach them. As a result, many new adjunct faculty are being hired to teach the new courses. Due to lack of resources and time, full-time faculty have not been able to properly train adjunct faculty. The administration has supported an effort to offer a training session and a small stipend to adjunct faculty. It is unknown if an ongoing program to train new faculty will result.

4. To date, articulation problems with the universities have been nonexistent with regard to the newly designed accounting courses at MCC. All state universities have agreed to accept these courses as equivalent to their own. However, articulation problems occurring in other areas have recently caused discontent between the community colleges and universities in Arizona. It is unknown at this time if changes may occur which negatively impact articulation agreements in the future.

5. Although it was hoped that assessment would be an ongoing process from the beginning of the AECC grant, the lack of administrative support in this area resulted in assessment of the accounting project not being properly planned and implemented. Accounting faculty were not trained in the area of assessment. Time and support were needed to develop a good assessment plan. Students began taking the new accounting processes in Fall, 1992. Therefore, the first potential graduates from ASU occurred in Spring, 1995. Despite faculty pleas for help in tracking this initial group of students, it was not until Summer, 1995, that the MCC administration made institutional assessment a priority. A tremendous amount of baseline information and feedback has been permanently lost.

6. Grading students for skill-based competencies continues to be a challenge. Most faculty have experimented with new and different ways to grade assignments each semester. Accounting faculty continue to collaborate not only with each other, but also with faculty in other disciplines such as English and Speech Communications. It was discovered early in the implementation phase that group grades only create more challenges. As a result, students work in groups, but are individually assessed. This creates a significant amount of grading for the instructor, but ensures individual accountability. It also solves the problem of forcing students to work outside the class in groups. This is a serious concern of community college students since many work full-time and have families in addition to attending school.

7. No perfect textbook exists to use with the new accounting courses. Several textbooks are currently being used. These books work well as references and for background material. However, as more faculty begin to teach the new courses, it is hard to dissuade them from allowing textbooks to be the driver of the course.

8. Many periodical articles are used to supplement the accounting courses. Copyright laws have made this a challenge. Most academic accounting journals are cooperative; however, other business periodicals have refused permission requests unless exorbitant fees are paid to reproduce articles for classroom use. Sending students to the library would solve this problem, but MCC's library is presently in need of resources for additional staff. Understaffing has resulted in problems which make it hard for students to obtain needed materials.

Unexpected Benefits from Change Activities

The most exciting benefit which has occurred from the changes implemented has been in student attitude. Student motivation, fewer absences, and lower attrition rates make teaching more enjoyable than it had been in the traditional accounting courses. A student comment often heard is that ACC230 or ACC240 "was the hardest class I took, but it was also the most enjoyable."

Increased respect from ASU faculty and staff has resulted because of the changes made by MCC. Often, potential MBA students are advised by staff at ASU to take the ACC230 and ACC240 courses at MCC prior to beginning the MBA program.

In Fall, 1995, the MCC management and marketing faculty requested that another new accounting course be developed for the two-year degree and certificate students in disciplines other than accounting. This course is currently being developed. It will be a three-credit course with a user focus, taught similarly to the ACC230 and ACC240 courses.

Measurement of the Effects of Changes Accomplished

As mentioned in a prior section, assessment has not been accomplished as hoped. Several assessment measures have been used and are summarized below:

1. Classroom research has been conducted on a continual basis since the first course offering of ACC230. Feedback from students is requested on a regular basis to determine the value of class discussions, team work, and effectiveness of assignments. The feedback received has been invaluable for purposes of continuous curriculum improvement.

2. Course and teacher evaluations are also conducted on a regular basis by peer faculty, the department chair, and the Associate Dean of Business. The written part of the evaluation filled out by students is dated, and the institution has not attempted to improve this document to meet changing classroom techniques. This type of evaluation offers only a minimal amount of feedback for the new accounting courses. The evaluations overall have been favorable, however.

3. The Dean of Instruction offered financial support in the Summer of 1995 to begin work on a more thorough assessment of the new accounting curriculum. MCC personnel have met on several occasions with ASU personnel to begin sharing information. It is hoped that a consistent effort on the part of both schools will result in information to help improve both programs. With the help of ASU, MCC was able to design and conduct a survey of students during the summer and fall of 1995. All students who had successfully completed ACC240 were mailed a survey. Of 256 surveys mailed, 62 students (24%) responded and 36 surveys were returned due to unknown addresses. Beginning in Fall, 1995, accounting faculty, with the help of the MCC Office of Planning and Research, will attempt to keep a file of permanent student addresses for future contact. The overall response from the survey was favorable. Of 62 students, 57 students indicated that they were satisfied or very satisfied with the new MCC accounting curriculum. Students attending ASU indicated they were well prepared for the ASU business program.

4. Attrition rates have been tracked in both the traditional and the new accounting sequence. For the academic year 1994-1995, 675 students enrolled in the traditional first semester accounting principles course, ACC111. Of this number, 321 students (47.5%) completed the course. During the same time period, 277 students enrolled in the new ACC230 course. The number of students completing the new course was 218 students (78.7%).

Special Insights from Carrying Out the AECC Grant

The AECC grant encouraged MCC accounting faculty to converse with each other on a regular basis. Valuable sharing of ideas has occurred. In addition, accounting faculty have been involved in campus activities to improve teaching and learning. This has encouraged interdisciplinary collaboration, which has also added value to the accounting program.

The MCC-ASU cooperative relationship resulting from the AECC grant should be a model for other disciplines as well as community colleges and universities nationwide. Articulation problems would not exist if faculty could work together toward quality education as have the MCC and ASU faculty.

The greatest outcome, however, has been the realization that students are capable of quality work. The new accounting curriculum demands a high level of performance from the student. MCC students have lived up to the higher expectations while maintaining a positive attitude. This, in turn, makes for a happier faculty.

Plans to Perpetuate the Changes that Worked Well

The ACC230, ACC240, and ACC250 courses will continue to improve. New ideas will be shared as more faculty begin to teach these courses. As evidenced already, other disciplines want to see the accounting faculty design new and better accounting courses for AAS degrees and certificate programs. The Office of Planning and Research has offered its help in properly assessing and therefore improving, the accounting curriculum. It is hoped that a permanent training program for adjunct faculty will be implemented. MCC faculty continue to disseminate information to their nine sister campuses, as well as to other campuses nationwide.

Major Reports and Articles Generated from Grant Activities

"Critical Thinking and the Introductory Accounting Curriculum," *American Accounting Association Communicator,* February, 1995, Charles E. Lewis, pp. 17-18.

Materials Available to Send to Others and How to Get Them

A packet of information including sample syllabi, handouts and exercises used in the new accounting curriculum can be obtained by contacting the Business Department at MCC.

Chapter 6
NORTH CAROLINA A&T STATE UNIVERSITY

Type, Size and Mission of Accounting Program

The mission of the Department of Accounting at North Carolina A&T is to provide a high quality learning experience in accounting education which effectively recognizes, appreciates and responds to the diverse background and abilities of our students. The academic and related programs of the Department are designed to provide students with the technical skills required for a variety of accounting careers and to provide opportunities for the development of the communications, analytical, and technological skills required for competitive performance in a diverse workforce and global economic environment. The Department's primary emphasis is teaching/learning with secondary and correlated emphasis on research and service.

The accounting program at North Carolina A&T is AACSB accredited and enrolls approximately 500 undergraduate students. The Department does not offer graduate programs. Students are admitted directly to the accounting program upon enrollment in the university. The Department has an extensive recruitment program designed to attract talented students with the potential for success in the field of accounting. The recruitment program is supported by an externally funded scholarship program. A competitive internship program is available to provide students an opportunity to apply their skills to practical accounting and business problems. Approximately 65 students graduate from the program each year. Placement of graduates is evenly distributed between public accounting and industry with a small number of graduates obtaining positions with governmental and not-for-profit organizations. Fourteen faculty positions are assigned to the Department.

Characteristics of Program Before the Grant

Prior to the AECC project, The Department viewed itself as being highly focused on the total development of students. Even though it viewed itself in this manner, there was no protocol to assure that the Department resources and efforts were focused in this direction. The Department tended to concentrate efforts and resources on the development of strong technical skills and provided minimal support and coordination to assure the development of communication, analytical, and social/interpersonal skills. While our recruitment program often involved personal contact with those being recruited, and our summer internship program gave students the opportunity to hone their communication, analytical and interpersonal skills, no organized method for monitoring and/or assessing these skills was in place. Additionally, there was no formal plan in place to ensure the enhancement of these skills in the context of classroom activities. The predominant method of instruction was the lecture method. This often resulted in instructors focusing on "covering the material" (via lectures) and the students relying on these lectures as the main means of acquiring an understanding of the concepts (rather than relying on themselves and their study skills).

Grant Objectives

Our goal was to enhance our existing curriculum by adding supplemental activities to each accounting course, so that our five specific objectives could be accomplished. Those specific objectives were: (1) to enhance professional awareness, (2) to improve communication skills, (3) to improve problem-solving abilities, (4) to enhance interpersonal, leadership and organizational skills, and (5) to promote computer-reliance.

Key Means of Accomplishing Grant Objectives

Efforts were made to involve all faculty in the change process. In all but one course, the activities for the course were developed by a team of two to four faculty members who either taught, might teach or were interested in the course and/or the material covered in the course. Membership on these teams was voluntary. After a given activity was developed, it was "tested" with a small group of students and subsequently revised before being used in all sections of the course the following semester. A second factor, which contributed greatly to our efforts, was the hiring of a communications specialist. This individual was hired in the first year of our project and was responsible for coordinating and helping to develop all communications assignments. She also gave assistance to faculty in the grading of these assignments, provided one-on-one assistance to students with these assignments, conducted workshops on writing skills, and was primarily responsible for our freshman activities. Faculty involved in the development of the grant-related activities/assignments were given either release time or supplemental funds to compensate them for their efforts.

Major Changes from Pre-Grant Conditions

The most significant change was congruency between departmental policies and procedures and the department's view of itself. This congruency has resulted in the establishment of a series of departmental programs and activities designed to enhance communications, social, professional and other skills. Prior to the grant, the department viewed itself as being focused on the total development of students while its activities and policies did not support this view. The activities associated with the grant have made the department realize the importance of formalizing a plan for making the total development of students a reality. Recognizing the complementary effect of soft-skill development on technical skills, and subsequently formulating and carrying out activities to foster this interaction, has also been an outcome. Further, the activities, policies and procedures established as a result of the grant have encouraged a camaraderie among administrators, faculty and students which recognizes and supports a broader view of the accounting education process.

More specifically, by developing activities which replaced and/or supplemented existing assignments in our accounting courses, we were able to target those skills we identified in our objectives. We added a required series of "mini-sessions" for our freshmen; required a minimum of two very structured writing assignments in our two Principles of Accounting courses, and gave the students in those courses guidance as to how the assignments should be prepared; required some type of writing assignment in all other accounting courses; added a lab to our Principles courses, during which time students are required to attend a minimum of two presentations/semester given by business professionals as well as to participate in a variety of other activities; made an introduction to case methodology a part of our Cost course; developed a semester-long project for students in Intermediate I; and encouraged the use of group assignments and cooperative learning in all accounting courses.

Methods of Achieving Faculty and Administrative Support for Changes

When we were notified that our proposal was chosen for funding, we began having faculty meetings which focused solely on how we would proceed with our project. Committees were formed to explore options for activities in each of our courses. While all faculty were given the opportunity to be involved in the development of those activities that would become a part of the courses they taught, some chose not to provide input at this stage. We recognized that faculty support is an iterative process which never reaches 100 percent. Patience and involvement were effective tools in obtaining the required support. In some cases we found that the enthusiasm of faculty who had tried and succeeded with new methods was all that was needed to convince others to change. Additionally, each faculty member's contribution to the grant project and/or to implementing the desired changes was one of the things discussed as individual faculty members formulated and finalized their annual plans with the department chair.

Administrative support for the project was obtained by making administrators aware of the importance of the proposed changes to the competitiveness of the accounting program and its students. Additionally, University and school officials were kept informed of the progress of the project and its anticipated benefits.

Change Activities That Worked Well and Which Others Might Copy

Because of their nature, all of our activities are readily adaptable to virtually all other accounting programs. While some do assume the student has been exposed to an earlier activity which may be considered a building block for that specific activity (for example, the writing assignments in upper-level courses assume the student has written at least one business letter and one memo in Principles), providing the necessary prerequisite for any activity should not be a burdensome task. Those that we felt worked well are listed below.

1. Freshman mini-sessions — a series of four one to one-and-a-half hour sessions conducted at various times during the freshman year. Each focuses on a skill we feel is necessary to a student's academic and professional success. The sessions we currently conduct are (a) an introduction to the department (of accounting) and the accounting profession, with emphasis not only on what will be expected of the student academically while at the University but also upon graduation and entrance to the workplace; (b) the importance of good communication skills; (c) study skills and time management; and (d) computer skills, including an introduction to the equipment in the accounting department's computer lab.

2. Writing assignments in Principles classes. By requiring the students to write both business letters and memos that focus on a technically difficult concept (for example, accruals in Principles I), students become familiar with two types of documents commonly prepared by accountants **and** gain a better understanding of the concept about which they are writing.

3. Principles lab sessions. By adding a lab to the Principles courses we are able to schedule presentations by business professionals which our students are required to attend. Thus, students are exposed to a variety of business topics as well as to business professionals. Also, this time slot gives us time to have students work on group projects in a supervised atmosphere.

4. Introduction of the case method in the cost accounting course. By introducing the case method during the first semester of their junior year, students acquire the skills necessary to tackle unstructured problems. Thus, after they work through a minimum of three cases in this course, where a heuristic is used to provide guidance, they are then better prepared to deal with cases in other courses.

5. Use of group assignments and cooperative learning. Fueled by information acquired at a cooperative learning seminar sponsored by one of the accounting firms, two of our faculty members tackled this area with gusto. After some initial disasters, both became enthusiastically committed to this tool. Their zealousness

(which was strengthened by their students' positive reaction to the use of these techniques) was contagious and other faculty followed suit.

6. A group assignment used in the auditing course. Our auditing students, working in groups, provide advisory services to a business operated by students in an elective course in the School of Technology. Each auditing group is assigned a different task, such as evaluating internal control, and must meet with the Technology students, analyze the problem, prepare a written report containing their findings and recommendations, and then make a formal presentation to the Technology students.

Change Activities That Did Not Work Well

Two specific project activities that did not work well were (a) the Intermediate I activity and (b) an assignment given in Advanced which involved working with a local small business. The former was a very ambitious series of assignments involving a business venture in a foreign country. The students researched different aspects of the country, looked at various accounting issues related to this venture, and then decided if the venture should be undertaken. All of this was done via written and oral reports and a final position paper. The lack of success of this activity was attributed not to the activity itself (students loved it and seemed to gain a great deal from it) but rather from faculty concerns about the amount of class time it took and the amount of time needed to create a new scenario and problems each semester. The Advanced assignment failed simply because of the logistics of working with an outside entity. Students found it almost impossible to meet with the business owner who, first of all, had a busy schedule the students had to work around and, secondly, required that the students come to him rather than him coming to them.

Another problem encountered was that of students being overwhelmed with group projects. As we started assigning group tasks (especially those which must be completed outside of class) we found that many other instructors in the School of Business were also making group assignments. The students who had several of these group assignments found it extremely difficult to schedule group meetings that were convenient to all involved.

While all faculty agree that the benefits students derive from the various activities introduced as a result of the grant are significant, many are still somewhat reluctant to use them in their classes. This is primarily due to the additional time most activities require — either in terms of preparation or grading. Additionally, for those activities that are done during class time, some faculty are still not comfortable with the fact that they may not have time to "cover" (i.e., lecture on) all the technical material they are used to covering in class.

Unexpected Beneits from Project

A major unexpected benefit derived from AECC grant activities is the socialization effects that have occurred. As a result of the freshman mini-sessions and the other group and professional development activities, accounting students have become a close knit group who are supportive of each other and the department. This is apparent to students, faculty and administrators external to the department, and is a source of considerable pride among accounting students. This socialization effect has also had a positive impact on faculty-student relationships. Students are now more acutely aware that faculty are interested in and supportive of their efforts and are willing to "go the extra mile" for them.

Measurement of the Effects of Changes Accomplished

We developed both formative and summative evaluation strategies as we worked through the grant. Because of the nature of our program and the grant-related changes, our assessments were of individual activities and skills rather than the accounting program as a whole.

Our **formative** evaluations were obtained primarily through questionnaires completed by students. We developed in excess of eight different questionnaires, with each focusing on a different aspect of the grant project. Generally speaking, feedback was overwhelmingly positive and supportive of the new techniques being used. Conversations with faculty also indicated that positive changes were occurring.

Most of the **summative** evaluation techniques/instruments that we had planned to use as we started working with our grant were later deemed to be inappropriate. Our instrument to measure knowledge of and attitudes toward computers, as well as the one to assess familiarity with basic facts related to the accounting profession, were such that students scored so high on the pre-intervention administration that there was little room for improvement.

We had originally planned to use a pre- and post-intervention assessment of writing skills by collecting a writing sample from entering freshmen and another from those same students during their junior and/or senior years. We later decided that this sample was not representative of the writing we were having them do, so we decided a portfolio evaluation would be better. As we collected students' work to put in these portfolios, we decided that the assignments were too varied to make meaningful comparisons. Thus, at this point, we have no quantifiable measure of the improvement in our students' writing skills. Informal faculty surveys do reveal, however, that faculty believe that our students are writing better as a result of the writing activities introduced as part of the grant project.

In one senior elective, heavy emphasis is placed on oral presentations. During two semesters, the videotapes of these presentations were evaluated using a 13-item checklist. Analysis of these results indicated the great majority of students showed significant improvement over the course of the semester.

Since no statistics (at least none in useable form) were available regarding the number and quality of applicants to the accounting program, number of dropouts, time taken to complete degree requirements, etc. prior to receiving the grant, no comparisons could be made between students in the program before the grant and those admitted after the grant was received. Additionally, since our "test group" graduated in May of 1995, they have not been out long enough to analyze their success on the job in comparison to students who graduated earlier.

Special Insights from Carrying Out Our Grant

As a result of our grant, we were forced to examine the way we delivered accounting education. We found that many of the things that we assumed were occurring either were not occurring at all or were not occurring with the frequency we thought they should be. Thus, our actions resulted in not just carrying out our objectives, but in reexamining our program in general. We can honestly say that the resultant changes have been and are beneficial and that a continuing quest for excellence has become part of our philosophy. It became obvious early-on that change comes at a significant cost and may not be readily accepted by all parties. However, we found that some of those who were initially most resistant to change became our most effective advocates of change. Finally, we realized that patience and commitment are essential to the change process.

Plans to Perpetuate the Changes That Worked Well

The activities related to the grant, along with other factors, made us aware that we needed a stronger system and/or policies for implementing and perpetuating these changes. We also anticipate that additional change will be necessary if the department is to continue to deliver a high quality educational experience to its students. As such, we realize it is necessary for us to have a system in place to ensure that ongoing assessments take place. Thus, we established a system of faculty committees and charged them with the responsibility of reviewing and encouraging change as is required for the department's various functions. To date, the committees have established protocols for change in their area of jurisdiction and are expected to become effective change agents.

Major Reports and Articles Generated from Grant Activities

"Introducing Practical Experience into Accounting Education," *Accounting Forum*, Vol. 18 #4, March 1995, William D. Cooper, Gloria Faucette, Charles F. Malone, pp. 69-78.

"Advisory Services Ltd: An Interdisciplinary Project Involving Accounting and Technology Students," *Mid-American Journal of Business*, forthcoming, William D. Cooper, Lynn Griffin, Charles F. Malone.

Enhancing Accounting Education, a comprehensive report of AECC grant activities published by the Accounting Department at North Carolina A&T State University, 1994.

Available Materials

Requests for information should be addressed to (Please note that a charge for copying and/or postage might apply):

Department of Accounting
School of Business & Economics
North Carolina A&T State University
Greensboro, NC 27411

Chapter 7
RUTGERS UNIVERSITY-NEWARK

Executive Summary

This project involves a revolutionary change in the training of graduate students for the accounting profession. The program focuses on an MBA education geared towards accounting with full integration of business and accounting subjects. Integration is obtained through topical integration and course coordination where topics of different disciplines broken down into basic units (coverage points) are brought together in an integrated framework.

Throughout the program a pervasive socialization program works on students' attitudes and skills aiming at forming a broad-based, tooled-for-life-learning professional. This professional, high in skills and positive in attitudes, will have a strong basic set of technical skills that will be acquired through a mix of teaching methodologies. The curriculum has an intensive "unfreezing" period, a body of "change," and a series of concluding experience to "refreeze" attitudes and skills (the "FLEX" program).

The project was planned to last four years, with the first class to start in May 1991, to be managed by different faculty members in its elements. Our current view is that the project is to continue indefinitely, on a constant progress and reevaluation. While curricular change showed itself to be a slow process, we feel that we have continued in the direction we had originally planned and adapted to what we are learning over time.

The Rutgers faculty continues to be committed to change. The influence of this program pervades not only our newly acquired Newark undergraduate programs, but also exerted major influence in the new MBA curriculum that was approved by the faculty and that came into effect in the Fall of 1997.

Type, Size and Mission of Accounting Program and Characteristics Before Grant

In 1957 the College of Business Administration on the Newark campus of Rutgers The State University of New Jersey graduated the first students in a new and innovative MBA program. This program accepted only non-business undergraduates who had taken no more than 9 semester hours of accounting in their undergraduate program. In the Professional Accounting MBA (PAMBA) program students received 27 semester hours of accounting and 36 hours of related business courses. Since that historic first class, over 1800 students have graduated from the program. At the school's last information survey conducted in 1986, 40% of the total graduates were employed in public accounting. Approximately 40% of the graduates were primarily in accounting or finance related positions and many had become chief financial officers and chief executive officers. The remaining graduates were employed in a wide variety of other occupations.

At the start of the change program, in terms of total hours and the split between accounting and business courses, the program resembled very closely the early curricula developed in the 1950s. Over the years the faculty has constantly updated the material in all of its courses to keep in step with new developments, teaching methods, and the microcomputer.

Objectives of AECC Grant

With the advent of the Accounting Education Change Commission, and the fundamental changes occurring in business, the School of Management decided that a very long and hard look needed to be taken at the content of the professional accounting curriculum, and that better articulation of the various subjects needed to be achieved. In addition to the basic cognitive knowledge that needs to be taught in the program, it was felt that students must be conditioned into certain skills of a non-cognitive nature never before part of an accredited college curriculum.

The GRAECE (Graduate Rutgers Accounting Education Change) project focused on the post-graduate market for accounting education. Post-graduate degrees in accounting are typically of two types: Masters in Accountancy and Masters of Business Administration (MBA). The first is typically an accounting specialization to supplement a baccalaureate degree in accounting, while the second entails an MBA degree with an accounting emphasis. This project focused on change within an MBA program with an emphasis in accounting.

The primary objective was to change the attitudes, skills, and methods of thought (unfreeze, change, and refreeze[1] of accounting students, accounting faculty, and accounting curricula). Throughout this project a methodology and plan has been implemented to achieve a series of specific objectives, including (1) lifelong learning, (2) integrated learning, (3) broad non-accounting background, (4) technological preparedness, (5) basic grounding in the methodology of learning, (6) Identification of and instruction in a basic set of competencies on which to build a foundation for lifelong learning, (7) internationalization of thinking, (8) construction of a basic set of skills, (9) development of a basic set of attitudes, and (10) preparedness for a vastly different teaching technology environment.

Figure 1 shows a comparison of the PAMBA program from 1969 to 1989 and the 1996 curriculum. Despite a series of changes, the program's structure is still similar. However, the introduction of the "defreezing and refreezing" periods, as well as the

---

[1]Schein (1961).

Figure 1

PROFESSIONAL ACCOUNTING MBA PROGRAM
CURRICULUM COMPARISON 1969-1989-1996

	1969		1989		1996
	First Term				
					Defreezing Period
3	Accounting Problems & Policy I	3	Accounting Problems & Policy I	3	Accounting Problems & Policy I
3	Aggregate Economics	3	Organizational Behavior	3	Organizational Behavior
3	Quantitative Analysis I	3	Marketing Management	3	Statistical Models I
3	Quantitative Analysis II	3	Financial Management	3	Financial Management
3	Marketing	3	Managerial Economics	3	Managerial Economics
	Second Term				
3	Business Law I	2	International Business	3	Financial Management II
3	Accounting Problems/Policy II	3	Deterministic Optimization	3	Deterministic Optimization
3	Auditing	3	Accounting Problems/Policy II	3	Accounting Problems/Policy II
3	Tax Aspects of Business	3	Tax Aspects of Business	3	Tax Aspects of Business
3	Cost Accounting	3	Management Info. Systs	3	Systems/Auditing
3	Quantitative Analysis	3	Business Law I	3	Business Law I
					Cost Accounting
	Third Term				
3	Accounting Problems/Policy III	3	Business Law II	3	Business Law II
3	Advanced Cost	4	Operations Management	2	Operations Management
3	Business Law II	3	Accounting Problems/Policy III	3	Accounting Problems/Policy III
3	Accounting Research	3	Auditing	3	Auditing
3	Finance I	3	Taxation of Business Entities	3	Taxation of Business Entities
	Fourth Term				
3	Accounting Problems/Policy IV	3	Accounting Problems/Policy IV	3	Marketing Management
3	Industrial Management	3	Cost Accounting	3	Advanced Financial Management
3	Marketing Cases	3	Advanced Financial Management	9	**The FLEX refreezing program**
3	ELECTIVE	3	Aggregate Economics		
3	Finance II	3	Business Policy		

extensive content changes and the emphasis on attitudes and skills, made the actual experience of the 1996 program very different from the earlier years. Considering the approvals necessary, and the experimental nature of our work, we decided to postpone dramatic course changes and focus on an incremental change process.

We invested great effort in revamping the principles of Rutgers' MBA program, changing the core requirements (reducing overall and introducing integrated core experiences), introducing the concept of tetrads (one unit courses), expanding the potential course offerings and increasing the opportunity for free electives. After intensive study and negotiation, we have a skeleton that allows all of our PA changes to become official under the MBA revamp umbrella. Consequently, additional faculty approval is not necessary, and we are proceeding to include in the school catalogs much of the change content.

> As usual, the PA program will lead the School of Management in educational change, and as usual we are going to be the first to face many additional difficulties and have to fine-tune our intended changes.

Specifics of the Change Process

A major program of change must aim at endowing an accountant with a certain set of attitudes and skills. Furthermore, to satisfy entry and progress requirements technical knowledge must be acquired. Students acquire these in educational settings by attending a formalized educational program that uses a certain set of teaching methodologies.

Attitudes

Essential attitudes to develop among students of accounting are:

Service: An attitude of service must be instilled in the student/professional. The nature of professional accounting work, whether public or private, requires a service orientation. The Rutgers Professional Accounting MBA advisory board found this quality to be lacking in accounting students.

Positive View of Business: Rutgers' PAMBA program brings in a majority of non-business school undergraduates. Part of the program's attitude change effort must concentrate on projecting a positive image of business and the people in business.

Ethics: Ethical issues and instilling a high sense of business ethics in accounting students became the issue of the eighties and will continue to be an issue into the next century.

Quality: Most major organizations now have quality programs in every area of activity. However, quality has not yet been recognized as an issue in accounting education. It is essential that quality be considered in the actual process of accounting education as well as an attitudinal issue in the preparation of entrants into the profession.

Lifelong Learning: An attitude of lifelong learning should result from the formal educational process. It is clear that a different set of skills and talents are required to be successful at different levels of a professional accounting career. Instructional programs can benefit by identifying a common starting core and designating further learning for different stages in personal development.

While our assessment analysis does not clearly show great changes in attitudes over the program period, we deliberately worked on these attitudes though discussion with the students in a large number of course situations as well as introducing many of these issues during the defreezing period.

Skills

The GRAECE deals with skill issues throughout all learning experiences in the PAMBA program, including the course work (cases and class presentations), the professional components (interviews, internship work) and the life on campus (toastmasters, business clubs, ethics lectures, student government). These skill issues include:

Integrative Ability: A good thinker must possess the following qualities: motivation to use thinking skills, a knowledge base, the ability to formulate and represent different points of view, and the ability to combine thought processes into workable strategies for problem solving (integrative ability). Integrative ability is of the highest order. Business problems and the detection of accounting discrepancies require the accountant, whether in public or private industry, to integrate issues from a wide variety of fields in many of which he/she has no specific competence.

Verbal Communication: A major criticism of accounting graduates is their poor communication skills. In the verbal communication area, students must be able to verbally express ideas and abstract concepts as well as explain in words numerical issues in accounting. Furthermore, the ability to make effective presentations to large or small audiences is also part of this skill and of great importance in the modern corporate world.

Writing Ability: In performing their managerial duties, accountants are required to write extensively. Both short management memos and in-depth analyses and news pieces are required. Also, in their letters to management, proposals to prospective clients, and briefs for legislative and judicial bodies, accountants must prepare clean, organized business communication of a specific accounting nature. Also, evidence shows that writing helps to develop needed higher order skills.

Ability to Work in Groups: Most audit field work is performed in teams with various aspects of the work distributed among the members of the audit team. Most audit review work is done hierarchically and decisions are made as "group decisions." Thus, group projects and group-based management simulations are important in accounting education.

> The enhanced communication skills of our students was one of the most observable positive results of the change effort.

In the Communications course, students were required to choose specific companies and prepare memos to top management throughout the defreezing period and first term. Oral presentations started there and went throughout the entire program, including many of the classes and the Flex program. Training and briefing students for the internship interviews and, later, job interviews, showed the effectiveness of this work as well as served as an additional motivational and training tool of great value.

In the Behavior and Policy course, faculty worked extensively with the students' personal skills, used a long-term corporate simulation computer game, and brought them into the FLEX program. These efforts had a strong focus on the accounting profession and on situations that students would likely encounter in their future professional life. The behavioral sciences course devoted substantial effort to the discussion of attitudes and the reinforcement of positive trends.

> In the students' views, the longitudinal exposure of the students to the behavioral and policy faculty made this non-accounting section one of the most positive factors of the change program.

Technical Background

Technical background skills entail a set of building tools on which the program will construct a wider set of technical and knowledge skills. This basic division allows for the allocation of learning throughout the program.

The initial period of the curriculum envisages an intensive unfreezing effect where, through cases and business discussions, issues will be raised on a wide variety of attitudes and skills. In this intensive period, students will be forced to question prior values and attitudes without an attempt to bring them to stability.

Through intensive instruction and drilling of the basics, efforts are made to ensure that all students have the basic building tools. The more advanced set of technical and knowledge skills are instilled throughout the entire program in most of its modules.

Computer Skills: The student/professional must be able to use a computer as a day-to-day tool. Under current technology, the student must be able to use word processing, spreadsheets, database packages, and must be able to access other computers through telecommunication.

Research Skills: Historically, a greatly neglected skill in our instructional process relates to the ability to perform research of a professional nature. These skills include literature surveys, accessing computerized databases, designing surveys and questionnaires, and analyzing these results.

International Skills: The internationalization of American business, as well as the strong interconnection of the U.S. economy with world-wide factors, requires that we prepare much more of an internationalist as an accountant. Skills of a general nature include the command of foreign language(s), awareness of geography, and awareness of cultural and religious differences. Specific to the accounting domain are the awareness of differences in accounting standards and the difficulties in measurement across nations.

Statistical and Mathematical Skills: Both statistics and mathematics (through calculus) are important in the development of accountants. Statistics, especially sampling theory and methodology, is necessary for Operations Management, Auditing, and Cost Accounting. Regression analysis is used in Cost Accounting, Marketing, Economics, and Finance. Mathematical models are used extensively in Finance, Operations Management, Economics, and Marketing. It is important that students possess basic skills in order to be able to learn the more advanced concepts in the instructional modules.

We worked extensively on the students' computer skills. At the inception of the program they were introduced to the needed tools such as basic operating systems, word processing, spreadsheets, databases, and the Internet and the World Wide Web. Throughout the program, they used PCs extensively in accounting subjects, systems, finance, etc. They also used computer games in behavioral science and finance. In our view, our students are very computer literate compared with our generic population, and we are continuing to educate the faculty so that they are able to educate the students, and integrate computer usage into their courses.

The Rutgers Accounting Web (RAW) has become the most visited accounting site on the Web, hosting major organizations such as the AAA, IMA, FASB, AGA, FEI and IIA. Several of the students participated in these efforts and most students, at the end of the last class, were Web literate and able to construct home pages and surf the Web in conducting accounting research. The RAW is part of the International Accounting Network that mirrors its content at several countries around the world and adds international content to its scope.

The work on the math and statistics requirements pervaded the last five years. We feel that the massive infusion of these materials in the defreezing period resolved a very serious problem that we previously had. While we continue to receive students with inadequate preparation, we now do not have a problem of cataclysmic proportions on our hands. Our students rapidly become competent enough in these areas to do well in courses requiring some quantitative skills. Our deep concern with this matter prompted changes in the procedures and rules of the entire Rutgers MBA program that are more realistic and well-balanced.

> We did not succeed in motivating our faculty to use international cases and to focus on transnational issues.

In the area of internationalization of our students, our results are modest. Moving the international business course to the last term provided a more mature student who was better able to understand the complexity of international issues. Many of our students (over 1/3 of the current class) are international, but our American students are mainly from New Jersey and have a very American focus. We are currently working on some of these issues with the help of our International Business area, and are trying to procure international Flex projects and international placement for our students.

Educational Program

Traditional course constructs in the PAMBA offer a large set of advantages in the reformulation of an accounting program. Issues such as faculty load, coordination, teaching days, skill set and preparation have been resolved over the years and have a momentum of their own. On the other hand, they also presented a set of difficulties and rigidities, particularly in relation to the traditional way of doing things and a long-term over-reliance on established textbooks and their coverage.

The GRAECE relied substantially on a modularization effort of the learning objectives and on the utilization of non-accounting courses to cover some essential accounting items that were also offered in other courses. Careful examination of the current curriculum (1996) and of a normatively desirable program of study indicated that:

> *Efficiencies Within Accounting Curriculum:* It is possible to eliminate approximately 20% of the current accounting course coverage simply by eliminating duplication in these courses. We did not manage to go this far. We have eliminated between 5 to 10% of the coverage that was redundant.

> *Efficiencies Within MBA Curriculum:* It is possible to move a series of accounting topics and issues to the basic MBA courses by using accounting examples to

cover these topics. Since GRAECE entails the redesign of non-accounting, basic MBA courses that are given exclusively to accounting students, coverage savings of an additional 10% is expected. We may have actually achieved a reduction of about 3-5% of these redundancies. Due to the efforts of our faculty colleagues, many of the illustrations in the quantitative sciences were of an accounting nature.

> Savings here are not measurable. It seems that some topics are elastic and if efficiencies are found, instructors tend to add new "essential" materials.

Efficiencies Resulting from Change in Emphasis: As the essential basic coverage is redesigned with an emphasis on lifelong learning and self-instruction, and a deemphasis on professional exam coverage as well as statute coverage, a smaller set of accounting topics will be needed. This also will allow an estimated 15% reduction in coverage.

These previously mentioned efficiencies were used to satisfy the needs of the new curriculum. The new focus allowed for the refreshing of the course content, the introduction of several computer games and simulations, and for the defreezing period. In the defreezing period, we incorporated an increasing emphasis on the accounting cycle and much discussion about the environment and the new accounting profession. We also managed to free some space for the increased emphasis on integration and, in particular, our very successful FLEX program. (See Appendix 1)

The Educational Program 1996
Defreezing Period

The defreezing period started with a two week "boot camp," with heavy time pressures and by this year, the 1997 class had four weeks of defreezing. The program is tailored to the students, and their quantitative instruction is the first emphasis. Computers, math and statistics are taught at the pace needed by each specific student and tutoring is available and used often. In the accounting cycle instruction we experimented, with great success, with the Sorter (events accounting) approach. Prof. Hillel Maximon adapted the approach to the PA students with great success, being elected as the best instructor by the 1996 class. While the boot camp nature of the first four weeks caused some problems, and is very hard on the faculty, several of whom volunteer for no compensation for the effort, we are firmly committed to its continuation. We feel that the building of team spirit and the defreezing of prior conceptions, as well as the pedagogic value of the materials, are of great value and make our program unique.

Modules and Decision Oriented Focus

While we still believe in this set of ideas, we found it nearly impossible to implement this in a pure form. Consequently, we attempted to integrate and modularize courses. The Systems/ Audit course sequence has been very successful. The faculty taught it in an integrated manner and sometimes even modularized it with other subject matter.

The Management Accounting / Managerial Economics sequence was, in our opinion, a great idea, and of great value to the students. The students however, felt it to be a bit demanding and a bit out of the domain of "real " accounting. The faculty did develop a valuable sequence of modules that we intend to continue to offer.

We continue working on the Finance/ Financial Accounting sequence. While we are very happy with the evolution of our Accounting Problems & Policy (I, II & III) sequence, the constant turnover of finance faculty made it very difficult to create major change. The Accounting Problems & Policy curriculum is now being integrated with Finance I & II.

The FLEX Refreezing Program

The Flex program was introduced two years ago and serves as the final refreezing experience where across subject integration and real-life consulting experience go hand-in-hand. Appendix 1 describes the main features of this program. The New Jersey chapter of the Financial Executives Institute and several national firms have cooperated with us on a major effort. Their ratings of the experiences are very high and it has been evaluated as a very useful effort from everyone' standpoint.

> Flex encompasses the AP&P IV course and the Policy course providing a real life consultancy effort for the students, bringing together the many diverse experiences and education from the PA program. It is different from the student internship in that it is mainly a cross-disciplinary experience in which students work in groups supervised by the faculty.

Teaching Methodology

The project objectives include the usage of a variety of teaching methodologies, including traditional teaching methods, experiential exercises, cases (integrative along different disciplines, illustrative of accounting issues and as a medium of transmitting real accounting/management experience), computer-based exercises and a wide range of other experimental pedagogical methods. These teaching methodologies have been used over the last five years and require not only great investment by the faculty, but also constant replenishment of their knowledge and teaching materials. Many of these materials and experiences can be found at the Rutgers Accounting Web (http://www.rutgers.edu/accounting).

A Modular Approach to Accounting Education

Unfreezing, Moving (Change) and Refreezing

The first stage of the process has to involve the unfreezing of attitudes in relation to former training and values. Students must be made to question the adequacy of their prior attitudes dealing with accounting issues and the other areas of attitudes discussed earlier in this paper. This is accomplished by two coordinated methods:

a) an intensive socialization and introduction period of four weeks at the start of the program; and
b) a series of cases and experiential exercises tailored to key attitudes in question.

A set of modified SEC enforcement cases is one of the tools used to raise difficult ethics questions where no course of action seems to be optimal.

The second stage of the process, lasting throughout most of the program, involves the moving of attitudes and the building of skills towards the desired direction. This stage encompasses the modular instruction process and the other peripheral activities.

The third stage of the process, during the last three months of the program, is the refreezing of attitudes, where the students are eased into the profession by a major increase of intensity of contacts with the profession and a large set of integrative activities. The **FLEX** program is the major device for this purpose.

The Case for Articulation in the PAMBA Curriculum

In every professional accounting curriculum, whether undergraduate or graduate, there never seems to be enough time to cover "necessary" material. Also, in these same curricula, very little is done to articulate material among the various courses. It is not possible at this time to exhaust the possibilities of articulation, but it is possible to cite a few examples. The full extent of meaningful articulation can only be carried out by means of a complete curriculum review and lengthy experimentation. The key focus is on accounting as an information function, with critical management decisions serving as the focal point of clustering CPs into modules.

Summary of AECC Assessment Efforts 1992-1996

Introduction

The February 1,1990, GRAECE proposal submitted to the AECC called for an assessment of the desired outcomes of the Rutgers change project. This section reviews the GRAECE assessment efforts from their inception in July of 1992 to date. The ensuing sub-section briefly reviews the research design and the rationale for it. The following subsection provides a synopsis of the data collection effort. The ensuing subsection reviews what we know so far about the outcomes while the final subsection describes what we yet need to understand.

Research Design

A longitudinal, pre- and post treatment, study of the progress of the professional accounting students through the accounting curriculum was used in order to control for personal characteristics that might affect student receptivity to the change curriculum.

- Questionnaires were administered to PAMBA students when they entered and left the program.

- The multi-year collection of data on successive groups of PAMBA students allows us to compare the effects of the Change implementation on student attitudes and skills from one year to the next, as that implementation unfolded from the Summer of 1992 to the Summer of 1996. Doing this may give us some limited insight into the relationship between specific identifiable changes and student reactions to those changes. While the multi-year examination of PAMBA students by itself allows us to understand 'treatment level' effects, a general MBA student panel also was used as a control group.

- Given that the purpose of the GRAECE changes was to enhance the students' capabilities, and therefore careers as professionals, we also collected data on the PAMBA students' post-graduation satisfaction with their careers and their retrospective satisfaction with the program.

Data Collection Effort Synopsis

As noted, a longitudinal, pre-post study design was adopted to control for the influence of personal characteristics on student response to the changes. The fact that the students who entered the PAMBA at the same time tended to finish the program at the same time made this design feasible, as did the willingness of PAMBA faculty to surrender class time for the assessment effort.

Entry and exit data was collected on the Change group classes that entered the program in the Summers of 1992, 1993, 1994, and 1995. We are able, therefore, to generate a comparison of profile gain scores between the students in the successive classes. We also collected exit data from the last pre-AECC PAMBA class that graduated in August, 1992.

Comparison data was also collected, using the same pre- and post-test, intra-person design on a population of General MBA students. Questionnaires were administered in class at the start of the students' careers within the Graduate School of Management.

Since general MBA (non PA) students do not proceed through their program in lockstep, and tend to interrupt their stays in the program due to part-time or full-time employment considerations, and follow very different specialization paths in their last semesters, we implemented the exit questionnaire by contacting the students repeatedly by mail and phone.

Twenty-seven of seventy-two individuals who responded to the initial in-class questionnaire in the Fall of 1992 and 1993 responded to the exit questionnaire, providing us with a response rate of 39%. We obtained information about the typical speed with which general MBA students progress through the curriculum. Based on the estimate that individuals typically take up to two years to leave the general MBA program after entry, exit questionnaires were mailed to students who took the Fall 1992 entrance questionnaire during the Spring of 1994. Students who completed the Fall 1993 entrance questionnaire received their exit questionnaires in the Spring of 1995. (Only entry data exists for students who entered the GSM in the Fall of 1994).

Consistent with the GRAECE proposal, repeated attempts also were made to contact PAMBA graduates at intervals of one and two years after their graduation from the PAMBA program. These contacts were made by repeated phone calls and letters. We sought to gain thereby some sense of their satisfaction with (a) their careers, (b) the profession, and also (c) their retrospective satisfaction with the Professional Accounting Program. Information on their professional development activities and views of the ethics of the profession were also sought. One year post graduation follow-up data was collected on (responding) PAMBA students who graduated in the Summers of 1992, 1993, and 1994. Two year follow up data on program graduates was collected on (responding) PAMBA students who graduated in the Summers of 1992 and 1993.

What We Know

A very preliminary analysis of the currently computerized data reveals that the program *significantly and positively* influenced the acquisition of a broad variety of technical skills. Values, however, were much less likely to show significant change in either a positive or negative direction.

The various data sets collected as part of the assessment efforts are currently being put into machine readable form. PAMBA student responses to the ethics case, for example, failed to improve significantly.

Over the five years that exit data has been collected from professional accounting students, the average overall satisfaction level with the program rose somewhat steadily. The last non-AECC change group's overall satisfaction with the program averaged 3.83 (n=18, S.D.=1.54). The group of professional accounting program students that entered the school in the Summer of 1995, reported an average satisfaction level of 5.56 (n=25, S.D.=1.00).

What We Need to Know

What we need to have is a detailed look at the pattern of changes in the levels of different values assumed by the variables over the course of the assessment project. This information, while interesting in itself, should be correlated with specific activities of the program in order to better understand what activities (e.g., student seminars, bringing in of outside speakers) may have had an effect versus those that did not seem to affect the educational outcomes experienced by the students.

Also important would be an analysis of any changes in the characteristics of the students attracted to the program; employer perceptions of changes in the quality of program graduates; information on the first and second time pass rates on the CPA exam, and how these pass rates have changed over time. All of these variables would shed additional light on the quality of the program. Also at this point, to the extent that these processes aren't normally carried out in the course of regular interchanges between faculty and students, there should be a series of focus groups led by neutral moderators to discuss the characteristics of the professional accounting program and how well the students believe that it tries to meet its proclaimed goal of fostering the values proclaimed as important in the 2/1/90 GRAECE proposal. Such focus groups would importantly assist in the interpretation of the quantitative data collected during the last five years.

Conclusions and Follow-Up Considerations

In conformity with its history of innovation in graduate accounting education, the Graduate School of Management is performing a revolutionary change in approach to accounting education. This proposal focuses on the graduate education MBA market and benefits from two key facts: (1) its students by-and-large come from a variety of non-accounting backgrounds leading to a much more eclectic product, and (2) all non-accounting courses are taught exclusively for the PAMBA program allowing for great control and change in its content.

The program attempts to unfreeze students' attitudes and skills, modify them according to a model of wide professionalization and refreeze them within a context in consonance with the needs of the future accounting profession.

The program encompasses a four-week intensive period where fundamentals are reviewed in a student-tailored mode and basic questions on the environment are raised. Students then go through a series of decision-oriented modules covering material from the stewardship function to the function of modern computerized information systems. Throughout this stage integration and methodology are explored in independent tracks while contextual and technical knowledge is administered. The final phase of the program encompasses a series of integrative experiences and the closing of a series of issues raised in the first part of the program.

The defreezing and refreezing efforts have been implemented as planned. The modularization of the curriculum has lagged and was implemented in a less dramatic format to avoid breakdowns in the process or major student/faculty turmoil. The realities of the system inertia made us more cautious, but with the new curriculum revision we expect to reach closer to the modularization of the curriculum.

The computerization of par tour our learning/teaching effort has ramped up to the extent that a substantial part of the curriculum uses forms of data processing support. The change project gave rise to the very successful Rutgers Accounting Web effort that also benefits Rutgers students, faculty and image. We continue committed to change and feel that is time to transmit some of our learnings to the accounting academic community. We expect our program of change to continue.

Materials Available to Others and How to Get Them

In addition to the internet availability of materials, interested readers may send requests for information to the Accounting & Information Systems Area, Faculty of Management, Rutgers University-Newark, Newark, NJ 07102-1895.

Appendix 1
Flex Program Description

RUTGERS

THE STATE UNIVERSITY OF NEW JERSEY
FACULTY OF MANAGEMENT

RUTGERS-FEI
PROFESSIONAL ACCOUNTING
FIELD LEARNING
EXPERIENCE PROGRAM
(FLEX)

Overview

The Rutgers Professional Accounting Program and the New Jersey chapter of the Financial Executives Institute (FEI) are cosponsoring a consultancy program that will provide our students with hands-on experience solving accounting-related problems in organizational contexts.

Goal of the Program

The goal of this program is to improve our students' ability to understand and respond to the information needs of decision makers in complex business environments.

Scope of the Program

Each participating company will provide a student group with an assignment to investigate a significant accounting-related issue that has potential strategic implications. This issue should provide students with an opportunity to wrestle with important questions, but should not expose the students to strategically sensitive information. The groups' deliverables will account for 40% of their grade in the Business Policy course and 60% of their grade in the Accounting IV course.

Procedures

1. Approximately half way through the spring semester, student groups will be formed and assigned by the faculty supervisors to the participating companies.

2. The supervising faculty members (Professors Cameron Ford and Dan Palmon) will jointly review the expectations and requirements associated with the project. The groups will be held accountable for a substantial amount of work *before the beginning of the summer semester.* This advance work is necessary to insure the quality of the projects and to give groups enough time to finish before the end of the summer.

3. During the remainder of the spring semester, the groups will collect the industry, company, and competitor information necessary to complete an effective profile of their respective companies' current circumstances. The specific form of this report, and the information resources necessary to complete the analysis, are described later.

4. Each group will appoint a representative whose role will be to serve as the primary contact person with their respective company. Participating companies must also appoint a representative who will facilitate their group's efforts to acquire internal information, schedule interviews, etc.

5. Each group will submit a detailed outline of their company profile, including copies of all supporting research materials, by **Friday, April 15th.**

6. Each groups' representative will schedule an introductory meeting, to take place no later than **April 29th.** Students may provide their company representative with the phone number (201-648-5511) of Cheryl Wagner, the Professional Accounting Program's Secretary, if they have no other means of receiving phone messages. This meeting must include their company's representative and their faculty advisor. The purpose of this meeting is to identify a viable issue to investigate, and to establish expectations regarding project scope, access to decision makers and documentation, deliverables, etc. If conflicts arise that prevent scheduling a meeting by this deadline, please contact Cameron Ford to make alternative arrangements.

7. Each group will deliver a one-page draft of their project proposal to their company representative and faculty advisor no later than May 6th. The final draft of

the proposal, taking comments from the faculty advisor and company representative into account, must be signed by all three parties and returned to Cameron Ford no later than **May 13th.**

8. When students return for summer semester, they will immediately begin making site visits in an effort to gather additional information directly related to their project. The company representative will help schedule meetings and provide access to relevant documents.

9. Once the projects begin to take shape, each group will submit two progress reports to their faculty advisor, the first on **June 17th,** and the second on **July 15th.**

10. Groups will present their findings on the Newark campus during a two-hour presentation at the end of the semester. A concise executive summary with supporting documentation and analysis will be distributed to the class one week before the presentation. Each group's company representative and faculty advisor are expected to attend the presentation. In addition, the groups will present their findings at the company's site if requested by the company representative.

Participant Responsibilities

Students

*   Submit a detailed outline of their company profile, including copies of all supporting research materials, to the supervising professors by **Friday, April 15th.**
*   Schedule, organize, and run the introductory meeting by April 29th.
*   Submit draft of project agreement by **May 6th,** and a final, signed copy by **May 13th.**
*   Submit two progress reports to the faculty advisor, the first on June 17th, and the second on **July 11th.**
*   Fulfill project requirements by submitting a written and oral presentation.
*   Act and dress professionally when meeting with company representatives.

Companies

*   Assign a company representative who is responsible for being the group's sponsor within the company.
*   Commit to project agreement presented by the student group.
*   Identify people who can provide useful information to the student groups, and help students to gain access to those individuals.
*   Provide access to relevant, non-sensitive financial and accounting information and reports.
*   Attend introductory meeting and group presentation.

Faculty Advisor

*   Attend introductory meeting and group presentation.
*   Provide frequent access to student groups in need of advise regarding both the process and content of their projects.

Suggested Company Analysis Report Format

This assignment is modeled after the types of reports that major accounting and consulting firms produce for their clients and for internal research purposes. All of the major methodologies utilized in strategic analysis are required to effectively complete this project. Students will also need to utilize most of the major business information sources available for public companies.

Major Sections

1. Industry profile including:

- Provide an overview that identifies and briefly describes your company's industry
- Identify the key players in the industry
- Assess the international competitiveness of the industry
- Conclude with an industry outlook that identifies trends, challenges, and opportunities

2. Company profile including:

- Name of company and affiliated businesses
- Current SIC codes in which the company operates
- The company's products
- A brief history of the company's development
- Financial and market highlights:
    Capitalization information
    Sales by product, sales by region, etc.
    Market highlights for each product including share, growth, and competitors' position
- A brief analysis of each competitor (i.e., name, SIC codes, financial and market highlights)

3. Problem analysis and recommendations:
- Problem statement
- Situation overview
- Goals and criteria to be met
- Recommendation including a description of the solution, an action plan and implementation concerns

4. Appendices:
- Source material references

Chapter 8
UNIVERSITY OF CHICAGO
GRADUATE SCHOOL OF BUSINESS

Type, Size and Mission of Accounting Program

The Graduate School of Business (GSB) at the University of Chicago offers both PhD and MBA degrees; the University does not offer business courses at the undergraduate level or undergraduate degrees in business. Both the MBA and PhD degrees offer concentrations in accounting; the MBA accounting program is accredited by the AACSB. Across all areas and in any given year, the GSB's PhD program has, in residence, about 60 students. The PhD program in accounting admits between one and four students each year, and, in any given year, there are about 12 accounting doctoral students in residence. Currently, the GSB offers four MBA programs: a full time campus program (approximately 1200 students), a part time evening and weekend program (approximately 1500 students), a domestic executive program (approximately 80-90 students admitted each year) and an international executive program (approximately 50-60 students admitted each year).

Students are admitted to these programs after an application process which screens on various test scores, grade point averages, work and other life experience, essays and interviews. Admission is selective; for example, the 1995 entering campus MBA class averaged GMAT scores of 660, GPA of 3.4 and 4.5 years of work experience. The student body is diverse; for example, 27% of the student body is international.

The major strength of the Chicago MBA program is its flexibility. Professors at the GSB are free to choose the teaching method most appropriate to the subject matter and their own teaching style. In addition, the program allows each student to construct a program to meet his or her own educational and career objectives. Importantly, the GSB imposes few core course requirements and permits students to elect, at their discretion, to satisfy a core course requirement with an advanced course in that area. Financial accounting, one of the four core courses, is taken by the vast majority of students; those who do not take introductory financial accounting substitute a course in intermediate or advanced accounting, financial statement analysis or one of the other financial accounting elective classes. All of the accounting courses are in high demand.

While a noticeable percentage of students accept accounting or auditing positions upon graduation, the typical MBA student in the GSB is pursuing a career in consulting or finance. Thus, the value of the accounting courses and curriculum rests largely on the ability of these courses to develop relevant skills, knowledge, and attitudes in individuals who will likely be *users,* rather than preparers, of accounting information. As described later, this feature of the program is also the central theme of the accounting change project.

Characteristics of Program Prior to AECC Grant

Like many accounting programs in the country, the GSB's had a largely preparer focus. That is, most courses focused on providing students with the philosophical and technical accounting knowledge underlying the preparation of internal and external accounting reports. Other accounting courses adopted a purely managerial approach, which while offering a stronger decision orientation often failed to provide a sufficient technical accounting component. Neither approach had substantial interdisciplinary content. In addition, courses tended to be structured around either financial accounting or managerial accounting, with few interdisciplinary links among the accounting courses themselves, to other functional areas (such as finance) or to other initiatives being taken at the school (for example, communication skills training).

Objective of AECC Grant

As indicated in our proposal to the AECC, one fundamental objective of our curriculum change efforts was to convert our accounting curriculum to a user orientation rather than the more traditional and, at the time of our proposal, more widely-adopted preparer orientation. The broad objectives of the new curriculum are to present accounting in a decision-making context, as part of the general managerial function, and to create sophisticated users of internal and external accounting reports. The specific goals of the GSB's AECC proposal were to design a curriculum which provides students with both substantial technical accounting content and a decision focus, to emphasize the environment in which business decisions based on accounting information are made and to teach research and communication skills.

In terms of the first two goals, our proposal to the AECC involved the development of new teaching materials — lecture notes, readings, problem sets, assignments and cases — to implement the user orientation. Existing materials, at the time of our proposal, tended to take either a preparer approach which does not provide a sufficient business decision component for our purposes, or a purely managerial approach which does not provide a sufficient technical accounting component for our purposes. The new materials, as proposed, were intended to focus on accounting topics from a business decision perspective.

The third goal of our new curriculum, as described in our proposal to the AECC, is the development in our students of teamwork skills, communication skills and skills in approaching, organizing and solving unstructured problems. The elective courses proposed to the AECC take a team project approach, provide increasingly unstructured and realistic problems and have formal mechanisms for providing separate feedback on the business communication aspects of student projects.

Means of Accomplishing Grant Objectives

The GSB accounting faculty had lengthy discussions about the deficiencies, in terms of achieving our overall educational objectives, of the preparer orientation of our accounting courses, both in general (that is, as a model of how accounting should be taught) and specifically (that is, as it applied to the development of accounting knowledge and skills to meet the needs of our students). In both cases, we believed that improvements in the traditional preparer approach were necessary and implementable.

The entire accounting faculty participated in the discussions and development of our new approach to accounting instruction. New faculty joining the GSB after the inception of curriculum change also participated in the project. Participating faculty included junior assistant and associate professors as well as senior tenured and chaired professors. These individuals taught courses in financial accounting, managerial accounting, auditing, strategic accounting issues, and international accounting. Faculty who developed new materials and new approaches implemented these changes immediately.

The project's implementation was supported by GSB deans and administrators, both in terms of supplying some faculty with release time and by encouraging the development of new elective and interdisciplinary courses.

Major Changes from Pre-Grant Conditions

The major changes provided by the project relate to (1) the financial accounting sequence; (2) the managerial accounting sequence; and (3) the development of strategic accounting electives.

(1) The financial accounting sequence consists of three courses: introductory financial accounting (BUS 310), intermediate financial accounting (BUS 316) and advanced financial accounting (BUS 317). To meet our objective of shifting the emphasis of the financial accounting curriculum from preparation to interpretation, changes were effected in each of the three courses. The degree of change varied with the level of the course: it is least for BUS 310 and most dramatic for BUS 317. For both BUS 316 and BUS 317, faculty developed and successfully implemented new course materials, including lecture notes, original cases and assignments. In addition, the BUS 310 course was adapted, with an international focus, for use in the International Executive MBA Program in Barcelona, Spain. Another feature of this international version of BUS 310 was the coordination of materials in this course with a concurrently taught organizational behavior course.

BUS 310 is substantially similar, in topical coverage, to introductory financial accounting courses taught at many business schools. An important difference is that, at the GSB and with the assistance of the AECC grant, it is now coordinated with BUS 316 and BUS 317. In particular, at the onset of the sequence, BUS 310 will prepare students for the user orientation to follow in advanced accounting electives. It differs from our elective courses in that it continues to stress certain aspects of preparation equally with interpretation, because we believe such knowledge is essential for sophisticated use of financial information. Further, because we believe that students' first exposure to accounting has a material influence on their decisions to take advanced electives in accounting and to choose careers where they will be heavily involved with accounting information, we have attempted to enhance that experience by institutionalizing specialized discussion groups for students in the first accounting course. The primary purpose of these groups is to allow for in-depth exploration of issues and concerns that could not be dealt with in sufficient depth and detail in the course of a typical class, review session or faculty office hours.

Both BUS 316 and BUS 317 take a highly technical user orientation. In addition, the topic coverage in BUS 317 deviates from the traditional coverage of advanced accounting topics to include emerging issues (for example, accounting for financial instruments) which require students to develop a proactive understanding of the application of proposed accounting changes to existing business organizations and transactions. This focus reinforces the notion that accounting standards are dynamic, and that successful business decision makers must contend with the evolution of the accounting environment in response to legal, political and economic forces.

(2) The managerial accounting sequence consists of BUS 311 (introductory managerial accounting) and BUS 315 (advanced managerial accounting). Our main objective in applying the user orientation to BUS 311 was to recognize that while few of our students enter careers in which they ordinarily prepare internal accounting statements, many, if not all, of our students become users of such reports; for example, in a variety of traditional managerial functions, such as production and marketing management, as well as in non-managerial functions, such as strategic and general management consulting, investment banking and litigation support. Our goal in BUS 315 is to use the knowledge and tools gained in BUS 311 to examine strategic uses of managerial accounting as part of the overall business decision system. Like the relation between BUS 310 and BUS 316 and BUS 317, we expect BUS 311 to provide both a basis for introducing the user orientation and the requisite technical knowledge to extend the user focus in BUS 315.

To achieve the goals of our new curriculum, our managerial accounting instructors have prepared lecture notes, cases and assignments which integrate the managerial accounting topics with concepts and issues in financial accounting, corporate finance, operations management, marketing and organizational behavior. BUS 311 was adapted for use in both the Domestic Executive and International Executive MBA programs. In the international program, BUS 311 is integrated with its companion course, operations management. A highly successful element of the implementation of these joint courses has been the requirement that each student prepares a final project in which he or she analyzes and solves a managerial accounting/operations management problem in his or her company. The students are also required to present brief summaries of these projects to the class.

(3) The strategy module of our accounting curriculum consists of six courses, all of which have been developed or restructured as part of the AECC grant: strategic analysis of financial reporting (BUS 410), taxes and business strategy (BUS 416), consulting applications of accounting techniques (BUS 418), international accounting (BUS 419), financial statement analysis (BUS 430) and the corporation and the legal/institutional environment (BUS 431).

BUS 410 provides students with the opportunity to view financial reporting decisions in the context of the organization's business strategy and from the perspectives of both managers and external parties. Through case analyses and discussions, the course emphasizes that accounting reporting decisions cannot be made in a vacuum and that judgments about the validity and appropriateness of alternative accounting measurement rules are inherently judgments about the relation between the organization's business strategy and the message communicated by the financial reports.

BUS 416, taxes and business strategy, offers students a general framework for thinking about how tax rules affect business decisions. The applications integrate concepts from finance, economics and accounting to achieve a more complete understanding of the role of taxes in business strategy.

In BUS 418, students apply (or study how others have applied) analytic techniques from accounting, economics, finance and statistics to various business problems in a litigation context.

BUS 419, international accounting, was developed in response to students' increased interest in international business. It exposes students, through lecture and case discussion, to the financial reporting regimes and accounting measurement rules that apply in different countries and considers the implications of these institutional arrangements for organizational forms and the structure of transactions.

Even prior to the AECC grant, BUS 430 (financial statement analysis) was a popular course in our curriculum. Over time, however, we have changed this course dramatically. For example, prior to our curriculum change activities, students often analyzed simplified datasets and reviewed some established empirical research relating to accounting and capital markets. As part of our curriculum change efforts, we have reoriented the course so that it trains students in conducting research into companies and industries and broadens the perspective from that of a financial analyst to that of a business decision maker evaluating the profitability of an industry, competitor, and acquisition or a recapitalization. The revised version of the course contains detailed teaching notes, problem sets, software and several cases.

BUS 431 is a highly interdisciplinary course (it is jointly offered as an accounting course, a finance course and a law course), co-taught by an accounting professor and a finance professor. The course brings together accounting, financial, legal and economic issues in the context of major business decisions, such as mergers, asset sales, spin-offs, leveraged buyouts and corporate restructurings. Several cases, dealing with securities litigation, proxy contests, restructurings and spin-offs, were developed for and are used in this course. An important element of this course is the requirement that students address unstructured problems (discussed in these cases) and arrive at their solutions using appropriate tools (e.g., event study methodologies). The class emphasizes the careful articulation of the business decision problem, sophisticated analysis to reach a defensible solution and a concise presentation of that solution; extensive feedback is provided to the students on their written solutions and their participation in class discussions.

Methods of Achieving Faculty and Administrative Support for Changes

The accounting faculty were unanimous in the decision to change the GSB's accounting curriculum, along the lines previously described, and to apply for AECC funding to facilitate that change. The University of Chicago Graduate School of Business has for many years been a leader in accounting education, and the University's emphasis on both research and instructional and curriculum innovation reinforced the changes which the accounting faculty wished to implement. In addition, the GSB's MBA program as a whole has increasingly emphasized the importance of developing habits and skills to support lifelong learning and of developing in our students the intellectual curiosity, teamwork skills and technical tools needed to thrive in unstructured and dynamic settings.

The changes in the accounting curriculum were also linked to other school-wide initiatives, including a program for Leadership Education and Development (LEAD) and various teaching seminars offered to faculty. Finally, the GSB and the University of Chicago as a whole have a tradition of encouraging faculty to be innovative in their thinking about research and teaching and of promoting interdisciplinary teaching and research. The changes made to the GSB's accounting curriculum are strongly interdisciplinary and, in some cases, are direct outgrowths of the research interests of the faculty.

Change Activities That Worked Well and Which Others Might Copy

(1) In general, the user orientation which was the focus of our change activities has been extremely well-received by faculty, students, employers and alumni. For example, while the GSB has long had a tradition of flexibility in teaching (with respect to both content and delivery of material), the AECC project has enhanced faculty awareness of alternative teaching methods. The grant also promoted substantially more experimentation with different approaches than would otherwise have occurred. While not all materials developed or approaches taken have been equally successful, the seed of continuous innovation in the classroom planted by this project has flourished and is a well-accepted aspect of each accounting course. Faculty are encouraged to develop and teach new cases and to include new topics,

and students welcome these experiments and eagerly participate in this process of change.

(2) The unifying user orientation theme among all accounting courses has translated into a highly integrated accounting curriculum. Not only are the accounting courses coordinated with one another, but they are also linked with courses in other areas within the GSB. The within-accounting integration is especially pronounced in the financial accounting sequence and in the managerial accounting sequence where the introductory courses (BUS 310 and BUS 311) provide both foundations for the user approach and the technical skills to expand this user orientation in the advanced courses (for example, BUS 316 and BUS 317 in the financial area and BUS 315 in the managerial area). The interdisciplinary integration is demonstrated by the development of several of the strategic elective courses, especially BUS 416 and BUS 431, and by the coordination of the managerial accounting and operations management courses taught in the executive MBA programs.

(3) While the accounting faculty used a combination of case discussion and lecture prior to the grant, the use of cases and unstructured projects, and the development of original cases and project materials, has increased dramatically since the inception of the project. In addition, several of the accounting courses now have detailed lecture notes which are extremely well-received not only by the students, but by other faculty interested in taking the course or preparing to teach that course in the future. Thus, the materials developed under the plan have lessened the preparation time that individual faculty members must devote to a given topic or issue. Students also find these materials to be extremely helpful in facilitating the learning process.

Change Activities That Did Not Work Well

As noted above, overall the change from a preparer to a user orientation was viewed as a success by all affected constituencies. The transition did not come, about, however, without substantial cost. Some of the challenges we faced during the transition process and still face include:

(1) Because of the substantial flexibility that individual faculty members have in their teaching, there are frequently different topics covered in different sections of same-numbered courses. In addition, in some cases similar topics are covered in different-numbered courses, although the approaches often differ. To the extent students are not able to sort out these differences in the coverage of material, this flexibility sometimes raises questions (in students' minds) about the content of one course relative to another. While the changes adopted in the accounting curriculum did not *cause* these issues to be raised (they existed well before our curriculum change activities began), to some extent the change to a user orientation magnified them by exposing students to the possibility that a similar issue may have very different consequences depending on its strategic and institutional context. Overall, we believe this ambiguity is an important element of real-world decisions and, therefore, we hesitate to impose more structure on course content.

(2) The focus on a user orientation places a heavier burden on the faculty in terms of both their pedagogical skills and their knowledge of general business issues. It is especially important to support junior faculty attempts to obtain these skills and knowledge in a time and cost effective manner. Toward this end, we have developed a standard set of teaching materials for the introductory financial accounting course which we encourage newly hired faculty to use, and to modify as they deem appropriate. After teaching these materials several times, junior faculty have successfully moved into teaching advanced elective courses. All accounting faculty are also encouraged to participate in teaching improvement workshops offered within the school and they are expected to attend related practitioner meetings, seminars and conferences, as appropriate to their teaching and research interests.

(3) Developing interdisciplinary courses and coordinating materials across functional areas are difficult tasks, in part because there are few rewards in the school's system for such extensive innovations. While the AECC grant has aided in this process considerably by providing financial support for release time and for the development of materials for such courses, we believe that these changes have only tapped the possibilities in these areas. An important challenge we face is how to encourage and promote even more interdisciplinary teaching and cross-area coordination.

Unexpected Benefits from Change Activities

The accounting curriculum at the University of Chicago has, for a long time, had a strong academic reputation. That reputation has increased with our adoption of the user orientation. Our MBA students bid for the courses they take, and given the few core requirements, this system provides a highly effective and independent means of assessing students' perceptions of the value of the accounting courses offered. While it is not always possible to isolate specific effects of the change activities on these perceptions, we note the following events which occurred since 1991 when we began implementing the change activities: on average, accounting courses receive the highest teaching evaluations of courses taught in the school; student demand for accounting courses consistently exceeds the capacity of our faculty despite yearly increases in the size of our group; the number of accounting elective courses has increased; the number of sections of both core and elective courses has increased; and six school-wide teaching awards have been won by accounting faculty, more than any other group in the school.

The materials developed as part of our change efforts have also had an unforeseen positive effect on the breadth and depth of information covered in individual classes. In contrast to the ex ante view that providing students with detailed lecture notes and assignments might detract from the value of the class discussion, we found that these materials heightened students' interest in the material and focused their attention on the more strategic aspects of problems. In short, faculty found that the use of these materials allowed them to expand the coverage of topics and the depth of analysis of individual subjects.

Measurement of the Effects of Changes Accomplished

Numerous methods have been and continue to be used to evaluate the effectiveness of our curriculum changes. These include:

(1) <u>Student evaluations.</u> It is the policy of the GSB to survey students in each class for their evaluation of the instructor's level of preparedness, the teaching materials and the content and organization of the course. The results of these surveys are published and distributed to students, faculty and staff. Many faculty also solicit qualitative written responses from students on both formal and informal bases.

(2) <u>Course registrations</u>. Because the GSB's curriculum has few requirements, course registrations provide an index of the success or failure of teaching innovations. This index allows us to measure relative performance, and also provides information concerning whether additional sections of certain courses should be offered in the future.

(3) <u>Self-evaluation and peer review.</u> On a continuing basis, the accounting teaching coordinator (a designated tenured accounting faculty member) works with the administration and the individual accounting faculty members to monitor the quality and content of instruction, and to suggest improvements and remedies proactively.

(4) <u>Surveys and focus groups for employers and alumni.</u> We consult with these constituencies on an on-going basis. The goal is to assess the perceived value of the accounting curriculum for our alumni as their careers develop. We also consult with employers of our graduates to evaluate the success of the new curriculum and to identify sources of additional improvements.

Special Insights Gained from Carrying Out AECC Grant

In the process of implementing changes to the accounting curriculum, the accounting faculty developed a much greater awareness of the range of materials and methods that could be used to convey both technical and strategic accounting information to students. The faculty also became more confident and more eager to try new, unproven materials and methods and to share the results of these innovations with others.

As a whole, the accounting faculty realized that the change process is carried out best, and perhaps only, when there is complete commitment from all members of the group. In our case (and as with many other AECC grant schools), there was complete agreement on the need and direction for change, and extensive involvement from both junior and senior faculty.

Finally, while it is not a special insight, the change process reaffirmed our belief that teaching and research are synergistic. These activities complement each other rather than compete for faculty attention.

Plans to Perpetuate the Changes That Worked Well

We believe that the overall change in approach from a preparer-orientation to a user-focus has permanently affected the way our faculty view the teaching of accounting. Materials developed by individual faculty members are shared with other faculty (here at the University of Chicago and elsewhere within and outside the United States). Indeed, it is that sharing that dramatically lowers the cost to individual faculty members of teaching new courses and ensures that successfully developed materials receive the broadest dissemination.

Faculty are encouraged to continue the process of innovation that the AECC grant seeded. For example, as part of the AECC grant, we instituted a teaching development program, coordinated by a senior tenured faculty member. The purpose of this program is to counsel junior faculty in their teaching and to consider how we could continue to develop the accounting curriculum to meet the changing needs of our students. This program has been very successful and has become a permanent part of the administration of the accounting group. As another example, the success of the coordinated interdisciplinary teaching of managerial accounting and operations management in our international executive MBA program has prompted a similar coordination in its domestic counterpart. At a more ambitious level, faculty in these areas are currently discussing the possibility of offering an experimental set of interdisciplinary courses in the campus MBA program.

Materials Available to Others and How to Get Them

Copies of the materials developed under the grant are available, at the cost of copying and handling, upon request.

Chapter 9
UNIVERSITY OF ILLINOIS
Project Discovery

Type, Size and Mission of Accounting Program

The University of Illinois, Urbana-Champaign (UIUC), founded in 1867, is a large land-grant, state-supported institution serving approximately 36,500 students, about 27,000 of whom are undergraduates. These students come from every state in the union and about 100 foreign countries. Approximately 92 percent of the undergraduate students are Illinois residents. There are ten undergraduate colleges, including the College of Commerce and Business Administration (CCBA) and one school at the UIUC. The CCBA has approximately 3,000 undergraduate students, 1,000 students in the various masters programs, and 200 in doctoral programs. The Department of Accountancy is one of four departments in the CCBA. The other departments are Business Administration, Economics and Finance.

Undergraduate education is strongly emphasized and admissions are highly competitive. The median freshman ACT composite score is 27 for the campus, and more than 25 percent of these students ranked in the top 4 percent of their high-school classes. Entrance credentials for students accepted into the CCBA are even higher.

Approximately 400 students graduate each year with an undergraduate degree in accountancy. In addition, approximately 40 masters students and 20 masters of tax students earn their degrees every year. The Department of Accountancy has been ranked first in the nation in *The CPA Personnel Report* (previously the *Public Accounting Report*) survey of accounting programs in each of the fourteen years in which this survey has been conducted. In addition, the Department of Accountancy was ranked number one by *U.S. News and World Reports* in its 1995 ranking of undergraduate programs.

The doctoral program in accountancy also is widely acclaimed with many of its graduates holding prestigious appointments in industry, government and at leading universities throughout the world. At present, some 20 students typically are enrolled in the program, with three-five students earning their Ph.D.s each year.

Characteristics of the Program Before the Grant

Prior to Project Discovery (PD), the UIUC undergraduate accountancy curriculum was typical of that found in large universities. During the mid 1980s, however, content and delivery shortcomings of the typical undergraduate accountancy educa-tion became salient to the UIUC Accountancy faculty. Among the problems identi-fied were that courses were rule and procedurally oriented, generalized and special-ized education were not integrated, there was no underlying conceptual framework which drew the various functional areas (tax, financial, auditing) together, students had become passive participants in the acquisition of knowledge, and many impor-tant skills (communication, dealing with uncertainty) were insufficiently addressed. Importantly, these shortcomings of accountancy education were not in any way local to the UIUC campus. In fact, accountancy students graduating from UIUC were among the most highly recruited in the nation. Nevertheless, it became clear that these shortcomings were threatening to diminish the value of the education students receive at Illinois and elsewhere:

> "... accountancy education does a poor job of instilling the requisite skills of discovery (problem identification, information search and evidence evaluation) that are critical to successful professionals in today's complex environment (University of Illinois at Urbana-Champaign, Department of Accountancy, *Project Discovery: A Prototype for Education in Accountancy.* A proposal submitted to the Accounting Education Change Commission, November 1990, p. 1)."

Central Objectives of the Grant

To address the shortcomings of undergraduate accountancy education, we aspired to create "... an innovative curriculum prototype that can be implemented at many universities around the country (University of Illinois at Urbana-Champaign, Department of Accountancy, *Project Discovery: A Prototype for Education in Accountancy,* p. 1)."

PD has these salient features:
- Active learning methods that enhance development of critical thinking abilities. The PD curriculum places much greater emphasis on methods and skills of inquiry, analysis, judgment and decision making.
- Accountancy courses that better integrate and reinforce general education requirements. The PD curriculum integrates, by extension and reinforcement in the major field, the content and skills learned in basic courses (e.g., English, Psychology, Economics).
- Introductory courses that are more interesting and broad-based. The PD sopho-more two-course sequence provides a broader introduction to business and an expanded understanding of the role of information in business and society.
- A conceptual framework that cuts across functional areas. Accounting courses in the PD curriculum are organized with an integrated conceptual structure com-mon to all aspects of the discipline. This conceptual structure emphasizes the utility of information, together with information production and dissemination given various uses.

- Better development and improvement of students' interpersonal and communication skills. These skills are reflected in the fabric of the curriculum through the
use of team projects and written and oral reports.
- Greater integration of research findings into the curriculum. PD courses include
knowledge gained through current research and related implications for the practice of accountancy.
- A working partnership between academe and practice. The goal is to enable a
continuous focus on the practical relevance of the educational process as well as
a richer and more contemporary flavor to the content of course materials.

Key Means of Accomplishing the Grant Objectives

A faculty committee met to consider how the identified shortcomings of undergraduate accountancy education could be addressed. We soon realized that pervasive
changes in the content and delivery of our courses was going to be required given the
scope of the identified shortcomings. Two other realizations interacted with this realization. First, we felt that because very few universities would have the resources
and credibility to initiate a comprehensive change to undergraduate accountancy
education, the UIUC faculty had an obligation to make our innovations usable at and
available to other universities. Second, despite our relative position, PD would be
served well by a strategic alliance with another university. Given the goal of producing a new accountancy curriculum usable on campuses other than UIUC, we
searched for a university with a different environment from the large, land-grant university environment represented by Illinois. Ultimately, we approached the
University of Notre Dame with a proposal that they join us in developing PD and
they agreed to do so.

A Director and Associate Director of Project Discovery were designated on both
campuses. Working under the PD Directors, a faculty committee developed the
structure of the new curriculum. Initially, responsibility for course development was
assigned to individual faculty members. These persons were tenured members of the
UIUC and Notre Dame faculties. Subsequently, faculty teams were asked to work on
each course. Coordination across courses and universities was encouraged by the PD
Directors and Associate Directors.

The tenured faculty members who were initially assigned primary responsibility
for each PD course were provided course teaching release time. These faculty members also taught the first offerings of these courses. The first sophomore PD courses
at UIUC were taught during academic year 1992-93 and the first class of 84 PD students graduated from UIUC in May of 1995. The University of Notre Dame followed one year behind the UIUC — their first class of PD students graduated in May
of 1996.

Major Changes from Pre-Grant Conditions

Unlike most other AECC grant initiatives, PD is a comprehensive change in delivery and content in all accountancy courses at the sophomore, junior and senior years. Perhaps the most significant delivery change involves the movement from an instructor-oriented to a student (team) oriented classroom. This change is related to our emphasis on active learning. In particular, we have operated under the premise that learning is more effective when students acquire (i.e., <u>discover</u>) knowledge by performing meaningful activities (or <u>projects</u>). Indeed, the name "Project Discovery" highlights our commitment to this view. The modal PD class, therefore, is not the sedate, instructor-in-the-front-of-the-room, lecture-oriented class typical of traditional courses. Rather, one finds in the modal PD classroom a relatively noisy, work-oriented environment in which students work as teams, debate among themselves, and present findings to their instructors and peers.

PD consists of three types of required accountancy courses:

1. A two-course introductory component taken during the sophomore year:

   - Accounting and Accountancy I
   - Accounting and Accountancy II

These courses place accounting in a broad context, introducing business concepts and practice and the role of accountants and accounting in society. These courses also provide a conceptual foundation for subsequent PD components. A key aspect of the conceptual foundation is the concept of <u>contracting</u>. Accountancy is presented as a discipline that facilitates contracting among members of society by developing, evaluating, and distributing contract-relevant information. Contracts involve two or more parties and these parties must make decisions regarding contract initiation, fulfillment and enforcement. These decisions, in turn, depend on information, and accountants play key roles in development, evaluation and communication of this information.

2. A five-course concepts component taken during the junior and senior years:

   - Decision Making for Accountancy
   - Accounting Measurement & Disclosure
   - Accounting Institutions & Regulation
   - Accounting Control Systems
   - Attestation & Assurance

In contrast with traditional accountancy education, which is organized around accounting contexts (e.g., financial reporting, internal reporting, taxation), these courses are oriented conceptually and around pervasive accountancy features:

Decision Making for Accountancy. One function of accountancy is to provide information to support informed judgments and decisions. Increasingly, accountants must comprehend and address the complexity, uncertainty, and ambiguity inherent in organizational settings while maintaining their role as effective decision-making facilitators. In this course, students learn to examine the decision-making implications of selected issues using ideas from economics, statistics, and psychology. Key course objectives include:

- Introduction to the uses of accounting information in decision making;
- Understanding the information needs of decision makers both inside and outside organizations;
- Development of judgment and problem-solving skills, particularly related to decision making in the face of uncertainty and ambiguity;
- Providing an integrated framework for structuring and using analytic models as aids to judgment and decision making;
- Understanding both quantitative and intuitive approaches to decision making, emphasizing their complementary strengths and weaknesses.

Accounting Measurement and Disclosure. This course focuses on capturing data underlying accounting information and manipulating and presenting data so that they meet the needs of contracting parties. Unlike traditional accountancy courses in which measurement and disclosure are presented in context-specific settings, a context-neutral conceptual orientation is used, thereby depicting how different settings affect the selection of measurement and disclosure techniques. Major course objectives include:

- Introducing measurement concepts including properties of measures, scales, allocation, aggregation and estimation;
- Identifying objectives of accounting information, including qualitative characteristics;
- Understanding valuation principles and alternative valuation techniques as they apply to both stock and flow measures;
- Understanding the relation between measures and decision objectives arising from explicit and implicit contracts.

Accounting Institutions and Regulation. This course focuses on the institutions that regulate the specification and application of accounting methods for different purposes. These institutions are both governmental (e.g., Securities Exchange Commission [SEC], Internal Revenue Service [IRS]), and private (e.g., American Institute of Certified Public Accountants [AICPA], Financial Accounting Standards Board [FASB]). They create regulatory and legal environs that have a widespread influence on accounting. Students acquire knowledge of these institutions and an understanding of how accounting rules, standards, and practices which they promulgate are used to address accounting problems. Other key objectives of this junior-year course include:

- Understanding the economic aspects of regulation;
- Examining regulation of accounting procedures with respect to external report-ing, including the activities of the FASB, the SEC, the AICPA, and, to a lesser extent, the Governmental Accounting Standards Board and the International Accounting Standards Committee;
- Considering regulation of accounting procedures for rate-setting and other pur-poses by governmental agencies and state public utility commissions;
- Examining regulation of accounting procedures for taxation including considera-tion of the US Congress, the IRS and foreign governments.

Accounting Control Systems. This course focuses on the mechanisms by which parties plan, execute, and monitor contracts. It covers the design of information sys-tems for facilitating and monitoring implicit and explicit contracts. Key course objectives include:

- Developing an understanding of the conflicting interests implicit in contracting settings;
- Examining controls (e.g., planning, transaction) which can be employed and considering factors that affect selection;
- Analyzing information technology and cost/benefit considerations in control system selection;
- Developing an understanding of information controls including those which assure completeness, reconciliation of independent sources, monitoring and ver-ification via audit trails.
- Balancing innovation and control.

Attestation and Assurance. This course is concerned with the lending of credi-bility by a non-contracting party to the assertions one contracting party makes to other contracting parties. The conditions which give rise to the demand for this ser-vice are studied and it is noted that they exist in numerous "places" within our soci-ety, including that of financial reporting. Also covered are services in which assur-ance is provided within an organization. An emphasis is attestation and assurance concepts including evidence, ethics, and control. Other topics covered include risks that the assure reduces and those that the assure bears. Key objectives of this course include:

- Developing an understanding of the role of attestation in a market-based econ-omy, including the potential subject matters of attest services;
- Examining concepts and issues of assurance, including assertions, risks and hypothesis testing;

- Developing an understanding of procedures for hypothesis testing, including the scientific method and the role of evidence;
- Developing an understanding of ethical dilemmas in assurance and attestation settings and an awareness of alternative standards and criteria for coping with these dilemmas.

3. A skills component taken during the junior and senior years:

- Professional Workshop

Recognizing that students pursuing careers in accountancy must develop numerous skills and capabilities and that some will not be sufficiently developed via the introductory and concepts courses, we have created this free-standing course. The Professional Workshop is a one-hour continuing course (taken for three semesters) which develops and improves skills required of a full-functioning professional including:

- Oral and written presentation/ communication skills;
- Teamwork and leadership skills including organization, negotiation and conflict resolution;
- Time management, stress management, and interviewing;
- Coverage of topics such as discrimination and other social issues of the workplace, cultural diversity and how to conduct business in a global marketplace.
- Applied research skills, database skills and Internet skills.

In addition to the required courses, there is a three course elective component:

- Financial Reporting Standards
- Income Tax Rules & Regulations
- Auditing Standards

These three courses are focused on professional standards. Relative to present accountancy courses, the PD courses described earlier are considerably less tied to the current rules of accountancy practice as promulgated in professional accountancy standards. While this altered orientation is purposeful, we recognize that students must acquire some understanding of the current rules of practice and, more importantly, a facility with the professional standards/literature sufficient for them to solve real-world accountancy problems. Instilling such an understanding and creating that facility are the goals of these courses.

Methods of Achieving Faculty and Administrative Support for Change

One of the most rewarding aspects of PD has been the commitment of the UIUC accountancy faculty to excellence and leadership in education. This commitment translated into strong support among the faculty for the PD innovations. Further, as we gained experience with the individual courses and the PD curriculum as a whole, the small number of faculty members who were negative or undecided became supporters. On December 8, 1995, the faculty of the Department of Accountancy voted unanimously to replace the traditional accountancy curriculum with the PD curriculum.

Prior to applying for the grant from the AECC for PD, we solicited the support of the Dean of the CCBA as well as the senior academic officer of the UIUC, the vice-chancellor for Academic Affairs (now known as the Provost). The letters of support from both of these administrative officers became important parts of our grant request. Similar letters were solicited and received from the analogous University of Notre Dame administrators.

One important feature of our development was that we did not immediately replace the extant traditional curriculum. Rather, as they were developed, one section of the sophomore courses and two sections of the other PD courses were offered on an "experimental" basis. Students then could volunteer for these sections. This approach was critically important to obtaining acceptance by the faculty because the traditional program at UIUC was so highly regarded. In essence, we did not ask them to take on faith that the newly developed courses and the PD curriculum as a whole would represent an improvement, but we made such improvement an empirical question. The empirical question was to be addressed via our program of assessment.

Change Activities that Worked Well and Which Others Might Copy

Our assessment evidence suggests that the PD curriculum is working quite well. We are, therefore, quite comfortable recommending that other institutions consider adoption of PD courses or the curriculum as a whole. Some individual features of PD seem to have worked particularly well and thus, are worthy of being highlighted.

An important PD feature is that the order in which accounting rules and concepts are presented is reversed relative to traditional programs. That is, PD students first are exposed to accounting concepts and then accounting rules. Moreover, when rules are covered, they are used as vehicles for elucidating concepts rather than as an end to themselves. This sequence and orientation seems to be a critical contributor to student perceptions of the field of accounting and, in turn, a major determinant of the interests and orientation of students who choose PD. If this continues, we will have impacted the "type" of student who majors in accountancy at the UIUC.

Perhaps the most common criticism of accounting students has been that they have weak communication skills. We have used a variety of means to address this criticism and in doing so have made oral and written communication skills a pervasive part of the PD curriculum. First, rather than deciding that responsibility was vested elsewhere on campus, the Department of Accountancy faculty took responsibility for enhancing our students' communication skills. Next, to leverage our efforts, we hired a communication specialist in a Lecturer capacity. In addition, support staff (e.g., law students, English graduate students) are hired to grade papers and meet with PD students. The communication specialist plays an invaluable role in helping faculty members weave communication skill exercises into the fabric of PD courses. The effect has been dramatic. In the modal PD course, multiple-choice exam questions have been virtually eliminated and written assignments are regularly graded both for content and the quality of written exposition. Also, students now have several opportunities to make oral presentations which also are graded for content and the quality of the exposition. As accountability has increased, so has student attention to these skills and in turn, their communication abilities have improved.

One important management tool is the matrix of knowledge, skills and attitudes which we developed based on *AECC Position Statement No. 1*. This matrix has been used both as a decision aid and as a tool for managing the curriculum as a whole. In the latter capacity, it has been especially valuable for assuring that individual PD courses would become an articulated curriculum and that we did not make serious errors of omission or commission.

Lastly, this report would be incomplete if we were not to highlight the importance of assessment in our endeavor. It already has been mentioned that it is difficult to imagine how a faculty (and other stakeholders) could be asked to change to a new curriculum without strong evidence that the new curriculum is an improvement. However, it also is important to recognize that assessment provides invaluable evidence for recalibrating in-process changes and for addressing the legitimate concerns of students who volunteer for experimental sections of the new curriculum. In the latter vein, an assessment program will work well if it fits the setting in which it must operate. In the case of the UIUC and PD, it was essential that the assessment program have scholarly integrity. Our assessment program, therefore, was informed by the education literature, and also rooted in psychology and social psychology theories and concepts.

Change Activities Undertaken That Did Not Work

There are three matters which belong under this heading. First, we made a mistake in the sequence that we used to obtain funding for PD. That is, we first sought funding from the AECC and, only after such funding was secured, did we seek funding from outside sources. It is likely that contemporaneous efforts for more complete funding of the PD innovations would have brought us closer to that goal. Related to this concern is that we underestimated the cost of building technology into PD classrooms.

In retrospect, another error was initial assignment of course development responsibilities to individuals. This approach seemed natural because historically course changes have been an individual and relatively private matter. We have learned, however, that while it is important that one person take a leadership role, a team approach provides insurance against the delays which can result from faculty departures which inevitably will occur when a development program extends over several years.

Lastly, it has been mentioned that PD was initially offered in a limited number of the sections of each UIUC accountancy course. While this approach was beneficial from a faculty acceptance perspective, problems arose due to the existence of dual accountancy programs. We underestimated, for example, the tension that would exist between students enrolled in the two programs. We can only speculate that rumors (e.g., about how good the new curriculum was and how well the PD students would perform on the CPA exam and fare in the job market) would have been reduced if we had more aggressively managed the transition process.

Unexpected Benefits

We did a good job of anticipating most of the many benefits that have accrued to the Department of Accountancy at the UIUC from PD. Perhaps the one exception is the extent to which PD students would be recruited by non-traditional employers of undergraduate accounting students (e.g., major investment banking houses). Similarly, the extent to which traditional employers would view PD students as competitors for positions otherwise offered to MBA program graduates was something of a pleasant surprise.

Measurement of the Effects of Changes Accomplished

We have designed and implemented an extensive and creative program for assessing the impact of the PD innovations. While students are enrolled in PD courses, this assessment plan has two broad foci. First, we evaluate students' self-efficacy (i.e., how much do students believe they know?). Second, we evaluate students' performance as a means of assessing their actual knowledge, skills and attitudes. Our extant evidence is:

1. Skills & Abilities: PD students are better at identifying accounting information resources and ethical issues than are traditional program students. Also, PD students are better at problem structuring and writing and they demonstrate higher levels of cognitive complexity in analyzing accounting issues. We have found no differences in the technical accounting skills of PD and non-PD graduates.

2. Self-Efficacy Judgments: PD students believe that they have stronger communication and interpersonal skills and weaker technical accounting skills relative to non-PD students at the UIUC.

3. Differences Between Students Choosing the PD and non-PD Programs: There are no significant differences in the ethnic composition of students who have, to date, entered the PD program relative to our traditional undergraduate accounting program. Further, we are unable to identify any significant demographic differences between PD and non-PD UIUC students, although PD students had slightly higher ACT scores.

4. CPA Exam Performance: Although PD was not directed at improving CPA exam pass rates, the first group of PD students' performed exceptionally well. Sixty-nine PD students took the May 1995 CPA exam and 32 passed all four parts — a pass rate of about 47%. This rate is substantially higher than the national pass rate and modestly higher than the rate (40%) at which non-PD UIUC students typically pass the CPA exam.

5. Job Placements: PD students have been in great demand by recruiters for both internships and permanent positions. PD students received significantly more permanent job offers, on average, than non-PD UIUC accountancy students. Further, the starting salary of the PD students was higher. Reports from 54 of the 84 May 1995 PD senior students indicate that 32 (59%) secured jobs with Big-6 accounting firms. Another four PD students secured jobs with regional public accountancy firms, making the total 36 of the 54 (67%) students. Eight of the 54 students secured positions with major corporations (e.g., Motorola, Baxter Medical, John Deere). Four of the 54 students secured jobs with nontraditional employers of undergraduate accountancy programs — major investment banking houses.

We also plan to assess PD students post graduation. Specifically, we have requested that the Chicago offices of all Big-Six accounting firms allow us access to the personnel records of all staff employees hired between June 1993 and May 1998. Specific data on which we intend to focus include personnel evaluations, promotions, salaries and job changes for PD UIUC graduates, non-PD UIUC graduates and graduates of other universities. To illustrate our expectations, relative to non-PD graduates, we expect that, in the work place, PD students will demonstrate better communication and interpersonal skills, and better problem-solving skills. Consequently, we expect PD graduates to advance more quickly than other graduates.

Special Insights from Carrying Out Our AECC Grant

We knew that PD would be difficult to implement. However, we underestimated just how time consuming and difficult implementation would be. But, we also grossly underestimated how rewarding PD would be. Virtually without exception, faculty who have been involved in the development of PD have indicated that they could not imagine the circumstances under which they could return to traditional undergraduate accounting delivery and content.

Project Discovery has better integrated our seemingly disparate roles as researchers and educators and focused us on the following core value: everyone in the university setting is engaged in learning (i.e., the acquisition of knowledge). Recognizing that everyone is involved in essentially the same activity has led to a closer and more collegial relationship between faculty and students.

Plans to Perpetuate the Changes That Worked Well

Following the unanimous vote of the accountancy faculty on December 8, 1995, we are working to obtain the various administrative approvals required for PD to formally replace the traditional accountancy program at the UIUC. We are not, however, presuming that accountancy curriculum innovation at the UIUC will be complete at that point. Rather, we recognize that efforts to improve our educational programs must be continuous.

Major Reports and Articles Generated from Grant Activities

Project Discovery was featured in the December/January 1996 issue of *Insight* — the magazine of the Illinois CPA Society (pp. 20-24). Articles are in process related to our assessment program and the results of that program. Bibliographic data on these articles are not presently available.

Materials Available to Send to Others and How to Obtain Them

Some of our materials (e.g., a program overview and course descriptions) are available on our World Wide Web site: http://www.cba.uiuc.edu/~accy/projdisc/. Course syllabi, illustrative teaching materials and further program details can be obtained by writing to the Project Discovery Director at the following address: University of Illinois, College of Commerce, Department of Accountancy, 1206 S. Sixth Street, Champaign, Illinois 61820.

Reference

Department of Accountancy, *Project Discovery: A Prototype for Education in Accountancy.* A proposal submitted to the Accounting Education Change Commission, November 1990, pp. 1-37.

Chapter 10
UNIVERSITY OF MASSACHUSETTS AT AMHERST
Three Curriculum Change Projects

Type, Size and Mission of Accounting Program

The Department of Accounting & Information Systems is one of four academic departments in the School of Management at the University of Massachusetts at Amherst. As the accounting program at the Commonwealth of Massachusetts' flagship University, our mission is to advance its goals and those of the School of Management. As part of a land grant and research institution, we are committed to providing higher education and public service. We do so by offering high quality educational programs that prepare qualified students for careers in accounting, related management professions, and academe; by creating and sharing new knowledge through faculty and doctoral research; and by providing outreach services to the Commonwealth of Massachusetts. Our aim is to be recognized on campus, within the larger University system, and throughout the state for leadership in the field of accounting. We strive to be the premier accounting program at a public university in New England and to be recognized for excellence among programs, public and private, in the Northeast.

The department's undergraduate program in accounting has approximately 120 graduates each year. About one-third of those graduates accept positions in public accounting, primarily with Big-Six firms. The School of Management has about 40 graduates each year from its on-campus masters program (Master of Business Administration and Master of Science in Accounting); usually six to eight of these students are in the Master of Science program. On average, two students are admitted each year to the doctoral program in accounting.

Our AECC grant concentrated primarily on the undergraduate level. Accordingly, the focus in the remaining sections of this report is directed to our undergraduate program in accounting.

Characteristics of Program Before the Grant

Historically, the department has had a traditional undergraduate program in accounting and its graduates have been well received in the marketplace. Nonetheless, we recognized before applying for the AECC grant that the skills demanded of accounting graduates were changing and that our curriculum had to change, too. Like many programs at the time, we believed that our curriculum was reasonably well designed to provide technical accounting skills to our students. However, we realized that inadequate attention was given to the development of expertise in the following areas: oral and written communication, critical thinking and problem solving, working in groups and making decisions in a group environment, and integration of the computer into the learning and decision-making process. In addition, we noted at the time that public accounting firms were beginning to hire an increasing number of students majoring in the liberal arts or the sciences.

Major Changes from Pre-Grant Condition

Our AECC grant concentrated on making curriculum changes in three different areas of our undergraduate accounting program. These changes are discussed in turn.

Accounting Course for Liberal Arts or Science Majors

This accounting course was developed during 1991. It has been offered at least once per year since January 1992. The course is available to students from the four liberal arts colleges in the immediate area, plus non-business students at the University of Massachusetts. A primary goal is to allow non-business students to consider careers in accounting.

The core activity is a three-credit financial accounting class taught in much the same way as an MBA-level first course in accounting (emphasis on interpretation of financial statements, with a lesser emphasis on construction of those statements). Other activities that have been used to supplement the course include workshops on additional accounting topics, a management game, and a field trip. To date, the most successful field trip has been to a stockholders' meeting of a medium-size company in Boston.

It should be noted that the main objective of this course is to attract nontraditional students (principally arts and science majors) into the accounting profession. In order to do this, these students must receive academic training in accounting and related areas. We expect this to be done at the graduate level. Accordingly, we have counselled each interested student to first complete his or her program of study in the arts or sciences and then apply to a graduate program in business or accounting. To date, a number of graduates of this accounting course have entered MBA or Master of Accounting programs.

Communications Course for Accounting Majors

This course, which focuses on both written and oral communication skills, was developed during 1990. A business communications consultant was employed to head up the project team.

The course was offered for the first time in the Fall 1991 semester. It continues to this day as a required course for all accounting majors. During the first two years, students met twice per week in large lecture sections and once during the week in small discussion sections. For the past three years, students have met three times per week in smaller sections (no more than 35 students). Despite changes in the way the course is delivered, the overall objectives have remained the same. A description of the current version of the course and its objectives is presented below.

The stated purpose of the course is to enable one to acquire and practice writing, thinking and speaking skills vital for effective performance in a variety of business environments. Writing assignments are used as a way to have the student think critically about audience, purpose and content, explore career development choices, become acquainted with business populations, and gain perspective on cultural differences in international business communications. A process approach to business writing is used in which the student is expected to (a) analyze writing constraints and decide on goals and purposes; (b) gather data, generate ideas, and organize content; (c) draft, rewrite, revise, edit, and proofread material, and (d) give and receive edits and responses to and from peers.

During the course, students are expected to write letters, memos and reports; give oral presentations; and interact in group projects. These assignments require the student to (a) construct arguments and gather evidence to support claims, (b) document their sources, (c) communicate and collaborate with others, (c) plan visual layouts for accessibility, and (d) think critically about tactics, tone, image, credibility, and international communications problems.

One full-time faculty member is in charge of the course. She is assisted by a number of teaching assistants (usually doctoral students from the English Department).

Computer-Based Modules for Use in the Introductory Course in Accounting

To date, we have developed the following computer-based modules that are currently used to enhance the introductory course in accounting:

A software case that demonstrates the effects of individual business transactions on the primary financial statements. Effects of transactions are shown graphically. The user may cover transactions in any order desired; a toggle function allows for repeated viewing of the balance sheet before and after each transaction. This case might be used by an instructor in class or by a student outside of class. The software case was constructed using Toolbook.

Two financial analysis cases. Each case involves computer-based searches for relevant company and industry data in Moody's Company Data — Academic Edition database. Results of the searches may then be downloaded into a Lotus file for further analysis. The cases are meant to be assigned for students to complete outside of the classroom.

Methods of Achieving Faculty and Administrative Support for Changes

From the beginning, the Dean of the School of Management and faculty members within the department have been supportive of the AECC project. As might be expected, though, some faculty were more strongly committed than others.

Faculty support was enhanced by providing monetary stipends to project team leaders and explicitly recognizing the efforts and accomplishments of project team members in the annual faculty evaluation process.

Another method of achieving faculty support was to engage two specialists (a business communications consultant and a person proficient with multimedia authoring software) in areas where faculty expertise was lacking. This minimized certain "start-up costs" that would otherwise have been made by department faculty members.

The Dean of the School of Management was particularly helpful by keeping the importance of the AECC project visible to the entire School of Management. In a similar vein, a campus visit by the Executive Director of the AECC, did much to demonstrate the importance of the project to the University as a whole. His individual meetings with project team members, the Dean of the School of Management, and the University Provost and administrative staff were extremely important to us.

Change Activities That Worked Well and Which Others Might Copy

We have identified six curriculum and pedagogical innovations that worked well for us. Any or all of them might be employed by those at other universities. They are:

1. <u>Integrating competencies other than technical accounting skills into the accounting curriculum.</u> These skill-based competencies include written communication, oral communication, working in groups, and critical thinking. While these competencies were first introduced in one or more of our AECC projects, they are found now in many courses in our curriculum (managerial accounting, intermediate accounting, systems, international accounting, and auditing). The establishment of the required communications course was the major catalyst in this regard.

2. <u>Using a team approach to curriculum planning and teaching.</u> As noted above, a team approach was used to accomplish each of our AECC grant objectives. This approach is now being used in other areas of the curriculum. Teams are currently being used to better integrate "clusters of courses." For example, we are currently using a team approach to better integrate material in the following four courses: introduction to computers, business applications of computers, systems, and auditing.

3. Integrating computer-based teaching modules into the curriculum. These modules were developed as an AECC project for the introductory accounting course required of all School of Management students. New computer-based modules are currently being developed for several other courses in the accounting curriculum.

4. Establishment of a Writing Center. There have been many benefits that have resulted from the development of the required communications course. One of these positive developments has been the establishment of a Writing Center. The Center is staffed by graduate teaching assistants and is available to all School of Management students.

5. Videotaping of students' oral presentations. A key ingredient in any learning experience is timely and effective feedback. We have become much more efficient in providing videotape feedback to students after they make oral presentations in our classes. This is done by using portable mounted cameras that are readily available in most classrooms.

6. Field trips to stockholders' meetings. One of the components to the accounting course we developed for liberal arts and science majors was a field trip to attend an annual stockholders' meeting. Student feedback was extremely positive. The experience provided external validation to many students that what they had learned in a classroom was relevant in the business world.

Change Activities Undertaken That Did Not Work

One of the initiatives proposed in our original grant application to the AECC was the establishment of a networked computer classroom that might be used by instructors in any of our accounting courses. For technical and budgetary reasons, we were not able to make the networked lab a reality. The initiative was subsequently scaled down to the development of computer-based teaching modules to be used in the introductory accounting course. Computer-based modules are currently being developed for several other courses in the accounting curriculum.

The idea of a networked computer lab with a common data base that might be used by a number of different accounting courses is still a viable goal. Recent upgrades to our computer facilities and the experience of faculty in making curriculum changes make this a likely possibility in the future.

Measurement of the Effects of Changes Accomplished

Effects of curriculum changes have been assessed by means of exit interviews of students, course and teacher evaluations by students, discussions with the department's Advisory Council, and discussions with faculty teaching the relevant courses. And, in the case of the accounting course for arts and science majors, we have also tracked graduates of this course to see how many eventually enroll in MBA or Master of Science programs.

Each of the projects was "fine-tuned" as we gained more actual experience with the specific curriculum changes. The scope and nature of written assignments in the communications course, for example, have changed over the years as we have learned more about students' skills and expectations.

Special Insights from Carrying Out Our AECC Grant

We have learned through participation in this exceptional program how difficult and yet stimulating change can be. While the outcomes of all of our efforts were not always exactly as planned, the grant has been a remarkable catalyst for significant and needed change. We wish to express our deep appreciation to the Accounting Education Change Commission.

Plans to Perpetuate the Changes That Worked Well

All of the changes we have implemented as part of the original AECC grant, in our view, have been successful. We are committed to retaining these innovations but within the context of continual improvement. Moreover, we are in the process of extending these innovations to other areas of our curriculum.

Major Reports and Articles Generated from Grant Activities

We filed four progress reports and one major summary report of our activities with the Accounting Education Change Commission. These are available to anyone who requests them.

Materials Available to Send to Others and How to Get Them

In addition to copies of the reports mentioned above that have been filed with the AECC, we would be pleased to send any of the following additional information to those who request it:

Syllabi for courses developed as part of the grant.
Course materials (assignments, cases, etc.) from any of these courses.

Please send inquiries to:

Dept. of Accounting & Information Systems
School of Management
University of Massachusetts
Amherst, MA 01003

Chapter 11
UNIVERSITY OF NORTH TEXAS
Integration of Classical Learning Core
with Professional Learning Core

Type, Size and Mission of Accounting Program

The mission of the Department of Accounting at the University of North Texas (UNT) is to maintain a leadership role in professional accounting education. The department will achieve this mission through the departmental objectives and strategies for teaching, research, and service. The primary educational programs of the department are the programs leading to an MS in Accounting. The programs provide students with the knowledge and skills initially needed for entry into careers as professional accountants. There is special emphasis on the use of technology and developing students' technological expertise. The programs help graduates become effective leaders in the accounting profession and contributors to the effectiveness of business, government, and other non-profit organizations. During the fall of 1995 the department had 153 students in the MS programs.

Another critical teaching objective of the department is to be a leader in the education and development of accounting educators in the United States through offering a high-quality doctoral program. Upon completion of this program, graduates are prepared to take an active role in the accounting academic community. In the fall 1995, the department had 20 students in this program.

A secondary teaching objective of the department is to provide a high quality BS in Accounting Control Systems for those individuals who do not enter the graduate program. This program is designed to prepare students for careers in certain industries and government entities which seek individuals with a strong education in business and accounting but without the degree of specialization provided by the integrated professional program. The program parallels much of the undergraduate portion of the five-year, integrated MS program, but is supplemented with additional credit hours at the undergraduate level.

Characteristics of Program Before the Grant

Although half of the 150-hour integrated program consisted of arts and sciences education, the linkage of accounting to the arts and sciences program was not threaded with a central core. Students took liberal arts courses without any reference to a central purpose. In the accounting portion of the program, lectures and problem assignments were the dominant teaching means. Although analytical skill was emphasized, students basically were conditioned to solve well-defined problems.

Central Objective of Grant

The UNT grant project calls for a logical linkage from the Classical Learning Core (CLC) to the Professional Learning Core (PLC). This linkage was established to accomplish the following goals:

- improve the knowledge base provided, especially with respect to general education and in understanding the way accounting relates to other disciplines.
- enhance capacity for independent learning — learning to learn.
- intensify the desire for continued learning.
- enhance communication skills — reading, writing, speaking, and listening.
- improve interpersonal skills and the capacity to work as a member of a team.
- upgrade competence in the use of abstract logic and the exercise of critical thinking.
- stimulate sensitivity to professional and social responsibilities.

UNT had in place a CLC developed by the College of Arts and Sciences in response to the Carnegie Commission's call for better integration of the core curriculum. The CLC program required six hours of English in the first year. Sophomore PLC students built on the freshman foundation by taking 18 hours, six each in English, history, and political science. All these courses were integrated under the central themes of virtue, civility, and reason, to which was added the theme of "accountability." The CLC continued the same learning themes in the junior year, culminating in a senior-year capstone seminar. A common set of "great books" was used in all of these courses.

Consideration of virtue includes relating contemporary moral problems to notions of virtue embodied in the classics of our cultural history. Civility concerns developing respect for the dignity of others and for rules that express a consensus for achieving a good life in pluralistic societies. Reason involves the two contrasting tendencies that consist of (1) the creative and speculative and (2) the technical and analytical. Accountability, the fourth element added to accommodate the needs of the PLC program, refers to the disposition of a person to accept responsibility for his/her actions in all facets of life.

The PLC portion of the 150-hour program included at least 30 hours from the existing CLC and 12 hours of economics and history/ethics. Existing mathematics and science requirements were continued. There were six hours of general education electives and each student also had 15 hours of electives in general education areas.

The PLC's key elements were (1) providing a solid background in general education, (2) integrating subject matter across courses both horizontally, within a semester, and vertically, from semester to semester, and (3) organization of subject matter around central themes. Putting these elements in place required extensive cooperation with faculty in the College of Arts and Sciences and extensive revision of accounting courses.

Key Means of Accomplishing Grant Objectives

The key to achieving the grant objectives lies in four areas: (1) support and commitment of the accounting faculty, (2) support of the faculty in the College of Liberal Arts and Sciences, (3) teaching material, and (4) support from college and university administrators at UNT. The cooperation of UNT's arts and sciences faculty evolved over a period of time before the grant was received. For a period of 20 or more years, the accounting faculty have been active and influential on this campus. They have taken part in campus-wide lecture series and other events, as well as many social and cultural activities that involve the university community. This interaction with faculties from other colleges created a situation in which the accounting faculty were known outside the College of Business and were respected for their contributions to the intellectual dimension of university life. The Department of Accounting was able to secure support from the Director of the CLC program in designing its grant application. Several meetings and seminars were held during the period of 1990-92, in which accounting faculty and arts and sciences faculty discussed the implementation of PLC courses with the central themes. Three joint two-day faculty retreats between accounting and arts and sciences faculty were held off campus where as many as 50-60 faculty members met to develop implementation plans.

The success of the AECC and other parties in exciting the accounting community, with regard to making massive changes in accounting curriculum and in improving pedagogy, had a significant effect on the PLC as implementation progressed. A new introductory text developed by the University of Southern California made it convenient to (1) adopt a user approach, (2) introduce the entire discipline of accounting quickly, (3) use student-centered pedagogy, and (4) intensify the development of interpersonal skills.

The implementation of the grant project coincided with a time of budget reduction in the university and a continuing decline in the number of accounting majors. The project put a great strain on the department's resources. While the university required the department to observe the policy of averaging 300 semester-credit-hours per faculty member, we had to offer PLC courses in a small class size. Fortunately, the department was encouraged by the central administration to continue the experiment regardless of the financial constraint.

Major Changes from Pre-Grant Conditions

The heart of the UNT curriculum change in accounting was to embrace the CLC as the essential liberal arts component of the program and to integrate into the PLC courses aspects of the same learning themes used in the CLC. The project also included some fundamental changes in how various parts of the accounting and business curriculum components were delivered.

In the freshman and sophomore years, PLC students were required to take the following CLC courses which were structured around the themes of virtue, civility, reason, and accountability:

Economics 1100 and 1110
English 1311 and 1321
Western Civilization (Hist 1051 and 1061)
Classical Argument (Comm 1400)
American Government (Psci 2041)
U.S. History to 1865 (Hist 2611)
Classical Argument (Comm 1400)

In the sophomore year, they took the first two PLC accounting courses (financial accounting and managerial accounting). A user approach was adopted for the two courses, with the first course designed so that students would understand financial statements without the use of the double-entry accounting system. The final part of the first course and the second course switched to the use of accounting information for making managerial decisions. Concern for the capture and compilation of information is delayed until the third accounting course in the program.

The "use of management information" (UOMI) segment began after students had completed an introduction to entity financial reporting, about two-thirds of the way through their first semester of accounting. At this point, students were familiar with an entity's financial and operating cycles, the three basic entity financial statements and how they related to each other, and basic financial statement analysis techniques.

The UOMI segment began with a review of the history and purpose of organizations. This tied in to parts of an economics course they took in their first university semester, as well as to their history and literature courses. This also allowed discussion of the Professional Learning Core themes of reason, civility, virtue, and accountability that continued to receive emphasis and reinforcement throughout the semester. Then, organizational needs for information were covered, including the role that accounting could play in serving those needs. The principal information need was to help plan future activities and predict future results of different sets of activities. The rest of the first accounting semester was spent describing and using cost-volume-profit techniques to quantify the expected results of planned operating activities, compare actual results to the plan, identify differences (variances), determine reasons for the differences and use all of this information to plan the next operating cycle's activities. The emphasis was on activity planning and measurement, and a series of cases were used. The cases started with planning a new service business, and continued through its first few operating cycles.

The teaching model in the second semester was to assign a reading/writing assignment on a subject before discussing it in class. Class time was primarily devoted to extending (rather than reiterating) the concepts covered by reading/writing assignments. The emphasis remained on activity planning and evaluation, rather than on financial planning/evaluation. The emphasis was also on the use of information to make decisions about the future rather than on the process of producing information from data.

Also during the second semester, students were divided into small groups (four or five students) and assigned a group research project. The goal of this activity was to learn about an assigned industry, identify the industry's principal revenue and cost drivers and relate them to the managerial information tools studied during the semester. Students prepared both written and oral presentations of their findings.

At the completion of the UOMI segment, students understood the structures, needs, and uses of information in business, the role of managers in an organization, the flows of revenues and costs in an organization, and the tools to help make decisions about future activities and evaluate results.

Following the second semester, students take a group of PLC accounting courses designed with similar learning tools, such as cases and team projects. These courses were:

Accounting Systems
Managerial Accounting
Intermediate Accounting
Professional Responsibilities
Taxation
Capstone Seminar

Beginning in the Fall 1994, the sequence of the first two accounting courses (Financial Accounting and Managerial Accounting) was reversed. The logic in teaching accounting to business students is to start from a micro perspective (activities within an organization) to a macro perspective (across the organization, i.e. firm-wide).

Methods of Achieving Faculty and Administrative Support for Changes

The accounting faculty at UNT had long been discussing fundamental changes in curriculum at the time the AECC grants were announced. A five-year program was implemented in the early 1980s. By the time of the curriculum change proposal to the AECC, the five-year program was flourishing and graduated more students each year than the undergraduate program. However, the accounting faculty were satisfied with neither the content nor the approach to teaching many of the individual courses in the accounting sequence, nor were they satisfied with the liberal arts component of our program. Even before the AECC grants, the accounting faculty were searching for ways to enhance students' liberal arts education while at the same time improving the business and accounting curriculum. At the same time, the accounting faculty became aware of criticisms of accounting graduates by employers as well as by various educational groups. Both groups felt that business curricula were too technical and restrictive. It was apparent that major restructuring was necessary in both accounting and business education.

In a situation where the faculty is dissatisfied with the current situation and where external constituents are also dissatisfied, the perfect opportunity for change exists. All that is needed is a catalyst to cause change. In the UNT case, the catalyst was the AECC. The decision to apply for the AECC grant was supported unanimously by all accounting faculty. As explained earlier, the accounting faculty had developed close relationships with the faculty of the College of Liberal Arts and Sciences and, consequently, they were able to get some key liberal arts faculty to join the effort to develop the AECC grant proposal and, later, to implement the proposal. Of course, the CLC program was a premier program in the university at the time of the AECC grant announcement, and the proposal to incorporate the CLC program into accounting education was welcomed by the deans of the College of Business Administration and the College of Arts and Sciences, and also by the provost and the chancellor of the university.

Change Activities That Worked Well and Which Others Might Copy

Although the experiment and assessment are not complete at this time, some preliminary judgments about the results have emerged.

1. We have gained sufficient experience to begin restructuring accounting courses for all our students. This will include coordination of each accounting course with non-accounting courses. We believe that these ideas about program change are transferable to other programs.
2. Certain features of the department's coordination efforts with the CLC program appear to offer opportunities for other programs. A strong alliance with the College of Arts and Science is essential for this type of project.
3. The user orientation to the first two accounting courses — Introduction to Financial Accounting and Introduction to Managerial Accounting — appears to be more effective than the traditional approach.
4. New teaching approaches, including extensive use of cases and student groups, appear to be more effective than the traditional lecture approach.
5. The emphasis on acquisition of communication, group work, analytical, and learning to learn skills can be achieved with the new teaching approaches.

Change Activities Undertaken That Did Not Work

Certain aspects of the experimental program have not worked well in the UNT environment. Since our environment is similar to many other public institutions, an awareness of potential problems can help other programs avoid these difficulties. Of specific concern are freshman-only admission, a full-time lockstep program, open admission, and four-hour courses.

The experiment required the department to recruit only freshmen into the five-year lockstep accounting program. The results suggest that it is difficult to recruit large numbers of students into a program like the PLC program as freshmen. Typically, "real" decisions about a college major are made only after one or more years of college study. The first accounting course is probably the most important for helping choose accounting as a major. Consequently, we need a program that allows students more flexibility.

Given the UNT student body, a lockstep program also creates major limitations. A large percentage of the students work and therefore take limited course loads. The lockstep program was one main reason for the high exodus of students from the PLC program.

The experiment called for open admissions. The goal was to determine whether a program like the CLC was feasible for all students. The "average" student appears to have particular difficulty with the CLC phase of the program. The accounting faculty do not believe that open admission is feasible. This concern appears to be pervasive across the CLC and is not limited just to PLC students. (Over 50% of the entering CLC students dropped out before the end of the first year.) The entire CLC program was replaced with an honors program in 1994.

The AECC proposal we submitted called for teaching four-hour courses in Accounting Information Systems, Managerial Accounting, and Intermediate Accounting. Due to various constraints, such as limitation of physical space and inflexibility of computerized course scheduling in the university, the four-hour course concept was very difficult to implement. Another difficulty encountered was the budget reductions in the university. It was costly to offer PLC courses which had only 10 to 15 students enrolled.

Unexpected Benefits

Several unexpected benefits have emerged from the AECC grant. First, the grant added additional credibility to the already well-known reputation of accounting programs on the UNT campus in the Dallas-Fort Worth area. A tremendous amount of respect for accounting faculty by other faculties and university administrators on the campus has been very visible. Second, the user approach to the first two accounting courses has generated a heated discussion among accounting faculties in the community colleges in Texas. A seminar course has been held at UNT during the summer for the past three years for community college faculty. The purpose of the seminar was to inform community college professors about the new approach to these courses at UNT and to encourage change in the community colleges. The reaction was generally favorable. Third, the AECC grant led to obtaining an additional grant from the Halliburton Foundation. Fourth, through the AECC project experiment, it was concluded that the first financial accounting course should be preceded by the first managerial accounting course. The faculty now believes that the micro-to-macro sequence is the proper way to teach accounting to all business majors, and that, in conjunction with the user approach, this sequence will attract more talented students into accounting programs.

Measurement of the Effects of Changes Accomplished

Four groups of students were admitted into the CLC-PLC program in 1990-93 with each group consisting of about 40 students. The first group graduated in December 1995. An outcome assessment will be performed on each group on their achievement of the purposes of the CLC-PLC program. At this time, the outcome assessment of the first group has not been completed. However, in the spring of 1994 (the junior year for the first group), the ten students who were still in the program were tested and the results are presented below:

Test 1 — A simple one-tail paired T test between the pre and post scores for the experimental group. This test was the first necessary condition for an experimental effect. The differences were substantially and statistically significant. But, obviously, the test is not sufficient. The difference could be attributed to maturation.

Test 2 — An F test of the differences and in the variances, covariances, and distributions of the experimental group and the control groups. The test was statistically significant and analytically substantive. Our experimental group had much smaller variance than the control juniors and seniors. Our experimental group differed significantly from normality while the other groups did not. This may indicate a differential mortality.

Test 3 — A multivariate regression (equivalent to a MANOVA) of the groups on the six raw (unpartialled) subset scores on the COMP. This test showed a difference between the experimental and control accounting juniors and seniors on most of the scales including the total COMP score.

Test 4 — A multivariate regression (equivalent to a MANOVA) of the groups on the six subset scores with the effects of the covariates (sex, ethnic group, GPA, SAT, English as the first language, and test effort partialled). This test showed nothing.

Test 5 — A multivariate regression (equivalent to a MANOVA) of the groups on the six subset scores with the effects of all the covariates except GPA partialled. This test was run on the assumption that some of the hypothesized effect might be embedded in the GPA. Partialling the GPA might miss the effect. This test showed a significant effect on the value clarification scale.

Test 6 — A multivariate regression on three groups (experimental, juniors, seniors) matched for GPA on the six sub-set scores partialled for all the covariances except GPA. This test showed significant effects. On the three scales, Social Institutions, Science and Technology, and Value Clarification, the experimental group was statistically and substantively different from the control juniors. They were not different from the control seniors. On balance, given the small sample, the results are interesting, perhaps even exciting.

By 1998, all four experimental groups will have completed their PLC program and data will be gathered on all four groups of experimental students. The first group of students indicated that the PLC program had prepared them well for their entry to an accounting career. The ten students in this group were placed in either accounting firms or major industrial firms.

Special Insights from Carrying Out Our AECC Grant

Several lessons have been learned from the experiment. The first important lesson is that teaching accounting with the traditional lecturing mode is not as effective as other teaching methods such as case study, group project, group discussion in class, class presentation, etc. Today, lecturing in class is no longer the dominate mode in teaching accounting classes at UNT. Second, the use of multiple teaching methods in class can make students think while they are learning — learning to learn. Communication skills, team work attitude, and work ethics also can be developed through a mixture of teaching methods. Third, students would learn accounting better — although there was no test to prove this point — without exposing them to how to prepare accounting reports at the beginning. Instead, they would understand accounting better if they could first learn how to use accounting information for various business decisions. Another very important lesson learned from this experiment is that a large number of students in the first accounting class do not have a good understanding of how a business firm operates in a competitive environment. Understanding the underlying forces behind business transactions has been wrongly assumed for students taking the first accounting course. To address this concern, the sequence of the first two accounting courses has been reversed, so that managerial accounting now precedes financial accounting.

Plans to Perpetuate the Changes That Worked Well

The lessons learned as described immediately above will guide future curriculum changes. Many additional curriculum changes have already been implemented. Communication skills, professional ethics, team work, analytical reasoning, professionalism, and accountability are now emphasized in accounting programs, based on the four themes of the CLC — virtue, civility, reason, and accountability. Also, the lecture method has been replaced with many tested and effective teaching methods. The experiment will continue and the faculty will continue to learn from it.

Major Reports and Articles Generated From Grant Activities

"An Analysis of Career-Relevant Skills Among Students at Different Stages in an Accounting Program," by Frieda Bayer, William Luker, Robert Michaelsen, and Neil Wilner. (Has been submitted to an educational journal for publication.)

"Curriculum Changes in a Professional Accounting Program: An Evaluation Model," University of North Texas Working Paper, October, 1991, by William Luker, Frieda Bayer, Barney Coda, Jr., Alan Mayper, and Robert Michaelsen.

"Project Report, 1995" Department of Accounting, University of North Texas, August 1, 1995. (This report was prepared for the Accounting Education Change Commission.)

Materials Available to Send to Others and How to Get Them

Copies of the above materials and report are available upon request. In addition, copies of course materials and syllabi for the PLC courses can be made available for the cost of copying. Any other reasonable request will be honored. Send your request to:

Department of Accounting
University of North Texas
Denton, TX 76203-6677
Tel: (817) 567-3077
Fax: (817) 565-3803

Chapter 12
UNIVERSITY OF NOTRE DAME
Project Discovery Accountancy Curriculum Project

Type, Size and Mission of Accounting Program

The Department of Accountancy at Notre Dame seeks to advance accounting education by providing outstanding educational experiences and programs for its students, by encouraging and rewarding meaningful scholarship of its faculty, and through extensive interaction with and service to its alumni, the Notre Dame community, the accounting profession, and society.

Accountancy has been an important major at Notre Dame since the 1960s. Notre Dame graduates about 1,900 undergraduates each year, and typically, about 200 graduates are accountancy majors. As a result, alumni of the program now number 6,000 and a large number of graduates are partners with Big Six firms or financial executives with industrial firms.

All Notre Dame freshman spend their first year in the Freshman Studies Program. They then choose their college as Sophomores and their major as Juniors. Usually, about 500 Notre Dame students enroll in the College of Business Administration each year and about forty percent of them become accountancy majors. However, presently College of Business Administration enrollment is at an all-time high, with the total Sophomore, Junior, and Senior enrollment at 1,700 students. There are no restrictions placed on students' choices of majors at Notre Dame.

The academic preparation of students admitted to Notre Dame is strong. For example, the average SAT score for the 1995-96 Freshman class is 1,240. Accountancy major scores are consistent with the university average. As a result, we have tried to design an accountancy curriculum that challenges students, and takes advantage of their capabilities.

A strategic advantage is that Notre Dame is truly a national university with students drawn from all 50 states. Given the high quality of the students and the fact that Big Six firms can recruit students for all of their major U.S. offices, placement of students in public accounting is strong, with about two-thirds of the Accountancy graduates accepting positions with Big Six firms each year.

Another strategic advantage is that Notre Dame has excellent teaching facilities. The university opened a new 75 room classroom building in 1992 that includes state-of-the-art technology. In the summer of 1996, the College of Business Administration moved into a new $25 million, 156,000 square foot building, located next to the classroom building. The two facilities combine to provide outstanding delivery capabilities.

Characteristics of Program Before the Grant

As is the case for many of the grant schools, Notre Dame accountancy majors were well-received in the market prior to the curriculum grant. The program was operating in a steady-state environment and content was heavily textbook driven. The mode of delivery was primarily lecture. A good portion of the class time was devoted to solving textbook problems. Most student assignments were individual as opposed to group-based, and a high percentage of the course grade was based on individual performance. The computer and other forms of technology were not heavily used for teaching and learning. As is the case with many steady-state programs, little consideration was given to program maintenance, the need for change, and program assessment. The quality of the instruction was perceived to be high, demand for entry-level hires was strong, and graduates were getting jobs.

Forces That Motivated Change

A variety of forces came together in the late 1980s to create what some called a "crisis" in education which motivated a new approach to education in general and for specific disciplines, including accounting. The crisis was explained most vividly by the National Commission on Excellence in Education in *A Nation at Risk:The Imperative for Educational Reform* (Washington, D.C., Government Printing Office, 1983), as follows:

"Our once unchallenged preeminence in commerce, industry, science, and technological innovation is being overtaken by competitors throughout the world. The educational foundations of our society are presently being eroded by a rising tide of mediocrity that threatens our very future as a nation and a people."

A Nation at Risk may have focused national attention on education like no other major event since Sputnik.

Within business education, the changing environment resulted in the AACSB re-engineering its accreditation processes and standards. The new standards were mission driven, focused on processes for continuous improvement, and were more intentional about performance measurement (assessment). At about the same time, The Carnegie Foundation for the Advancement of Teaching (1990), published its *Scholarship Reconsidered: Priorities of the Professoriate,* by Ernest Boyer. The report supported a broader definition of scholarship to include the scholarship of teaching. The report caused many business educators to rethink their definitions of high quality scholarship and to focus attention on the relation between research and teaching.

For accounting educators, additional forces were at work. The American Accounting Association's Committee on the Future Structure, Content, and Scope of Accounting Education (The Bedford Committee, 1986) issued its report which called for an expanded view of accounting education. Shortly thereafter, the (then) Big Eight firms issued their own report: *Capabilities for Success in the Accounting Profession.* The report was followed by funding of $4 million that enabled the establishment of the Accounting Education Change Commission and provided the resources for change.

At Notre Dame, the time was also ripe for change. The College of Business Administration hired a new dean in 1989 and a new Department of Accountancy chairman in 1990. Also, the university was investing heavily in technology and new teaching facilities were on the horizon. Within the Department of Accountancy, retirements and other factors resulted in great change in the composition of the faculty. New people brought with them new ideas and the enthusiasm to support change.

Key Means of Accomplishing Grant Objectives

The AECC grant was for *Project Discovery*, a joint project of the University of Notre Dame and the University of Illinois at Urbana-Champaign. The primary objective of *Project Discovery* is to produce an innovative curriculum prototype that can be implemented at many universities around the country. In working to achieve this objective, we:

*Developed and implemented a new two-semester foundation course in accounting and accountancy.

*Developed and implemented a complete accountancy curriculum for junior and senior accountancy majors.

*Are producing dissemination documents that we call "Course Studies" to facilitate implementation of *Project Discovery* at other universities.

*Are engaged in a variety of assessment activities.

Some two years before the development of the Project Discovery proposal, a group of accountancy faculty members at the University of Illinois began meeting to consider developing a new curriculum along the lines of the Bedford Committee recommendations. Later, the Illinois team traveled to the University of Texas at Austin and engaged in similar discussions with a small group from that accounting faculty. Based on all of these discussions, the concept of the *Project Discovery* curriculum emerged. Eventually, a proposal was written, submitted to the AECC, and partial funding for the project was approved.

In June, 1991, some 50 educators from Notre Dame, Illinois, and area colleges participated in a conference on teaching and learning, held in South Bend. Sponsored by the Arthur Andersen Foundation, the conference featured presentations by leading educators on topics such as the environment of teaching and business education, critical thinking, active learning, and technology. Articles from the conference have been compiled in *Critical Thinking, Interactive Learning, and Technology: Reaching for Excellence in Business Education,* edited by Thomas J.Frecka (Arthur Andersen & Co., 1992).

Unlike the other AECC projects, **Project Discovery** is a combined endeavor of the University of Illinois and the University of Notre Dame. Both schools set up faculty committee structures to oversee the project. Project directors were named, teams of faculty members were assigned responsibility for developing individual courses, and subcommittees were assigned to other project tasks, such as the development of assessment plans.

Major Changes from Pre-Grant Conditions

In designing the new curriculum, we were guided by the following beliefs:

*Students must become critical thinkers and take a more active role in the learning process. They must develop the self-initiated skills of discovery that enable a lifetime of continuous learning and growth as a professional. To do so, the curriculum needs to place greater emphasis on methods and skills of analysis, judgment, and decision making.

*General education requirements, and the skills developed therein, should be better integrated through extension and reinforcement in the major field.

*The accounting curriculum should be integrated, using a conceptual framework that cuts across accounting subspecializations and that stresses its information production and dissemination role in society.

*The foundation course of the accounting curriculum, which serves both as a broad introduction to accounting (the system of organizing, evaluating, and disseminating information) and accountancy (the professional activities of the accountant), should be more conceptual and less technical. It should produce an understanding of the relations among accounting, business, and society.

*The frontier knowledge gained through research must be effectively incorporated into the learning process of accounting students.

*A closer working partnership must be forged between the academic and practicing communities to develop a learning environment that is more representative of the technological and discovery features of the practice environment and to create richer materials for classroom use.

The first ***Project Discovery*** course was offered to a group of 150 students at the University of Illinois in fall, 1992. As planned, Notre Dame has lagged Illinois in implementing the curriculum by one year. The first Project Discovery course was offered to all College of Business Administration students (550) at Notre Dame in fall, 1993.

The Contracting Theme

An explicit objective was to consider contracting notions throughout the curriculum. We believe that a broad-based contracting perspective provides considerable scope for discussing accounting issues, measurement and disclosure considerations, standard setting, and other dimensions of the role of accounting in society. In addition, the contracting view facilitates learning the interrelationships among many aspects of business activity and, in turn, facilitates learning of accounting.

The Planned Project Discovery Curriculum

The intent of Project Discovery was to design and implement a complete sequence of accounting coursework to take the place of the then existing accounting curriculum.

The following framework for the accounting core was proposed:

Introductory Component:
Accounting and Accountancy I and II: A two-course Sophomore sequence designed to (1) provide an introduction to business concepts and business practice; (2) provide a comprehensive overview of the uses of accounting information and the role of accountants in society; and (3) provide the conceptual foundation for in-depth study of the entire accounting sequence.

Accounting Concepts Component:
The intent was to develop five courses that would provide an in-depth understanding of the pertinent aspects of accounting. The five courses are:

Decision Processes and Accountancy: A course focusing on the science of individual and group decision making.

Accounting Measurement and Disclosure: A course intended to develop concepts of measurement and information disclosure required for decision making and contracting.

Accounting Institutions and Regulation: An examination of the institutional, regulatory and legal environment in which accounting information is used.

Accounting Control Systems: An examination of systems for facilitating and monitoring the set of explicit and implicit contracts that control the activities of organizations.

Attestation: An examination of the independent public accountant's attest function.

Skills Development Component:
The intent was to develop a series of one credit-hour workshops that would focus on the development of relevant interpersonal and communication skills.

Comprehensive Integration Component:
The intent was to develop an Accountancy Practicum course as a means of comprehensively integrating all of the skills and knowledge gained in the rest of the Project Discovery coursework.

The Actual *Project Discovery* Curriculum at Notre Dame

For a variety of reasons, the actual *Project Discovery* curriculum at Notre Dame is somewhat different than the proposed curriculum. First, in developing the proposal, it was envisioned that additional accounting coursework dealing with professional standards would have to be provided. Also, a separate taxation course was not developed as part of the project. As part of the actual development, we incorporated additional coursework into the project. Second, at the same time Notre Dame was implementing *Project Discovery*, it was planning to start a masters degree program in accountancy. As part of this planning process, it was determined that a course like the Accountancy Practicum was better positioned as a fifth-year course. Third, resource constraints prevented us from fully developing the skills workshops. Further, we felt that many of the oral and written communication skills, team building skills, and lifetime learning skills were being developed in the other *Project Discovery* courses or business communication courses already offered by our business school. Later, we were pleased to receive a grant from the Ernst & Young LLP Foundation to support the development of Communication and Leadership coursework. Pilot coursework was offered for the first time in the spring, 1996 semester. Finally, course developers at Notre Dame proceeded somewhat independently of their Illinois counterparts. By lagging Illinois in implementing *Project Discovery* courses by one year, they had the benefit of the Illinois experience as well as their knowledge of what made most sense for Notre Dame.

Today, the actual Notre Dame accountancy curriculum (required courses for accountancy majors) consists of the following (3 credit-hour) courses:

Sophomore Courses (Required for Business Majors)
Accounting and Accountancy I
Accounting and Accountancy II

Junior Courses (Required for Accountancy Majors)
Accounting for Decision-making and Control
Accounting Measurement and Disclosure

Decision Processes in Accounting
Accounting Institutions and Regulation

Senior Courses (Required for Accountancy Majors)
Accounting Information Systems
Advanced Accounting Measurement and Disclosure
Federal Taxation
Attestation

No problems arose as we sought support for the project at the college level. Discussions were held with the college's Undergraduate Curriculum Committee. The project's objectives were viewed as consistent with the educational objectives of the college. Since the project would not involve a shift in resources between departments, other departments would not be harmed. One benefit of the discussions was the development of a greater awareness of the content of the principles of accounting and introductory finance courses. As a result of the discussions, some overlap of material between the courses was eliminated.

Faculty members, the dean, and members of the accounting profession were invited to visit the first *Project Discovery* classes. This helped to develop additional buy-in. Supportive comments from members of the profession and feedback they provided to students about the importance of the skills we were trying to develop were additional motivating factors.

Notre Dame was one of the few major accounting programs that did not have an advisory board. Shortly after the project commenced, we were able to form an advisory board. Meetings with the board, including sessions with students, provided another means of communication.

Our approach for enlisting student support was to not promote *Project Discovery* as a revolutionary change, but instead, we treated it as evolutionary progress in achieving our mission of providing outstanding educational experiences for our students. The chair had already established a student advisory group and periodically met with that group. Small groups of students were invited to meet with individual course instructors as another means of communication.

Status of Project

As planned, we started implementing the new curriculum in the Fall semester, 1993. Two *Project Discovery* courses, Accounting Institutions and Regulation, and Attestation, were taught to large groups of students for the first time in 1995-96. The first class of *Project Discovery* students graduated in May, 1996. Readers should keep in mind the "in process" status of the project in evaluating its effectiveness.

Documentation and Dissemination

The faculty approved a documentation and dissemination plan that is in the process of being implemented. A committee was formed to develop the documentation plan and to oversee its completion.

Documentation consists of the following:

(1) **Course studies:** Documents we call "Course Studies" are our primary dissemination tool. An individual course study includes a course summary, statement of learning objectives, syllabus, sample exams, and sample course materials. Included in all course studies is a matrix that links assignment material to both accounting content objectives and to skill development objectives. Course studies are being distributed free of charge to interested parties.

(2) **Teaching plans:** Individual class session teaching plans have also been developed. These plans are linked to the matrix and course summaries provided in the course studies.

(3) **Teaching notes:** More detailed guidance concerning individual assignments is provided in teaching notes. The teaching notes include suggested solutions for the cases and problems developed for the project.

Type (2) and (3) documentation are available for a small fee to help defray copying and mailing costs.

As an additional means of dissemination, a *Project Discovery* conference was held in the fall 1996. Representatives from about forty universities attended the conference where the content of the Illinois and Notre Dame curricula was presented.

Assessment

Assessment involves the systematic collection, interpretation, and use of information on student characteristics, the learning environment, and learning outcomes to improve student learning. An Assessment Committee was formed to develop our assessment plan and to monitor its implementation.

Prior to *Project Discovery,* elements of systematic assessment were already in place for the Department of Accountancy. Multiple groups — students, individual faculty members, an elected faculty committee called the Committee on Promotions and Tenure, and the department chair — are asked to assess the effectiveness of individual courses and faculty. At the end of each course, students also provide "Teacher/Course Evaluations" using a university-designed instrument.

Accountancy majors also complete a Senior Survey during their last semester. Our recent response rate has been one hundred percent. The survey documents placement experience and also includes questions evaluating the quality of accounting education at Notre Dame, including both positive and negative aspects of the student's experience.

The faculty assesses learning outcomes through exams, homework, research papers, classroom presentations, class participation, etc. At the end of each course, faculty members also complete two reports. The first report, called the Instructor's Course Evaluation Summary, provides open-ended responses concerning: (1) major features and innovations used in the course; (2) evaluation of the success of the course; and (3) planned changes for the next time the course is taught. The second report, called the Skills Development Summary, asks the faculty member to identify course objectives and the procedures used to accomplish them. This is the "matrix" referred to earlier under "Course studies." To the extent a given course has multiple sections and instructors, the teams meets to develop a common matrix.

Program/curriculum assessment builds on and complements these assessment efforts within individual courses. In-class assessment techniques allow the teacher to monitor teaching effectiveness and make mid-course corrections. Such intra-course measurements enhance learning by actively involving students in assessing their own learning. They also encourage faculty to experiment with and vary their teaching techniques. Commonly used tools include informal discussions with students and short, mid-term open-ended requests for feedback. More formal tools are increasingly coming into use including classroom assessment quality circles, self-diagnostic learning logs, one-minute papers, and directed paraphrasing.

Our planned Curriculum Assessment Program is summarized in Appendix 1. Note that the program identifies specific cognitive, behavioral, and affective goals and specific learning objectives related to these goals. Specific assessment measures and the timing of the measures are also identified. In assessing *Project Discovery* at Notre Dame, again it is important to point out that the project remains in process and that we are just beginning to implement our assessment program.

What We Have Learned and Future Challenges

Almost overnight, the Notre Dame accountancy program went from a steady-state environment to an environment of great change. In addition to the AECC curriculum project, other changes included the hiring of fourteen new faculty members over a five-year period, the establishment of two chaired professorships, greater expectations for faculty scholarship, an AACSB accreditation review, new teaching facilities, faculty approval to begin a masters degree program in accounting, and discussions about starting a doctoral program.

In an academic environment of great change, success depends greatly on maintaining faculty morale. We believe that morale will remain high if the faculty believes it is doing important work and if it is rewarded for that work. One reason *Project Discovery* is succeeding at Notre Dame is because that faculty believes it is important. Undergraduate education at Notre Dame always has been and always will be extremely important. The Accountancy Department knew that if it wished to maintain its leadership position in accounting education, change was necessary. It, therefore, supported the original concept of *Project Discovery* and modified that concept to make it fit at Notre Dame.

During this time period, we also improved our system for evaluating faculty performance, primarily by asking the faculty to provide more documentation. For example, in the past, teaching was evaluated based primarily on the Teaching/Course Evaluation input provided by students. Now faculty document their development activities and provide a great deal of detail about their courses.

During this time we have been able to increase faculty summer support for research and for curriculum development activities. Faculty Fellow appointments have been established with each of the Big Six firms. Several faculty members have received prizes in recognition of outstanding teaching. In cases where senior professors are no longer active researchers but remain outstanding teachers, we have been able to increase their teaching loads and provide them with greater rewards for their teaching. Assistant professors receive a semester release from teaching after their initial three-year contracts are renewed. Although Notre Dame does not offer sabbaticals, we do have some flexibility in course load assignments, and it has been possible to provide some faculty members with reduced teaching loads while they are involved in heavy coursework development activities. Finally, the university has remained fiscally sound and has provided a competitive level of faculty compensation. All of these factors are part of the reward structure that impacts faculty morale.

We have **learned** the following as a result of *Project Discovery*:

1. Textbooks have become more like reference books as faculty members write more of their own materials and utilize materials from a variety of sources. At the same time, there is a greater tendency to tailor instructor-developed material to specific textbooks so that a change in textbook requires more work than in the past.

2. Coordination between classes and courses is a key to success. We have designated a faculty coordinator for each *Project Discovery* class. The instructors for multiple-section courses meet on a regular basis. We also have periodic meetings with the entire faculty to communicate progress on the project. Five years ago, the faculty would have spent little time on such activities. Today, and in the future, curriculum coordination will remain a time-consuming faculty activity.

3. Teaching takes more time. It takes much more up-front planning and more day-to-day planning. In addition, there is more grading that needs to be done and assignments have to be more creative. Some graded assignments can be used only once or twice before extensive modification is needed.

4. Research findings can be used to greatly enrich accounting education at the undergraduate level. For example, research related to the contracting and

informational roles of accounting provides structure for much of our financial and managerial accounting coursework.

5. Documentation has a great deal of value, but it also takes a great deal of time. Too many documentation requirements can create disincentives.

6. Student group projects raise honest issues that weren't present in the past. For example, instructors need to be very explicit about what is acceptable communication between groups. They also need to be explicit about expectations concerning the individual's participation as a full member of the team. In this regard, it is important to use peer evaluations. The form that seems to work best for us is one that asks group members to state explicitly what work they did on the project.

7. Students are much more computer literate than they were in the past. Spreadsheets, databases, presentation software, and e-mail are commonly used tools. It has not been necessary to spend much time teaching basic knowledge of these tools in upper level courses.

8. Students ask broader questions in class. They seem to have a better understanding about how accounting relates to business.

9. There is much more student participation in class. This makes it more difficult to plan how long it will take to cover material, especially the first time a new course or a new assignment is covered.

10. While the scholarly reputation of the faculty as a whole has improved greatly during the *Project Discovery* timeframe, primarily as a result of new faculty hires, the research productivity of course developers went down during the development stage.

11. Working with the faculty of another university presents some difficulties. Distance, different mindsets, different environments, and moral hazard problems make coordination and the sharing of information difficult. Having said this, it is clear that the joint Illinois/Notre Dame curriculum project benefitted both faculties. *Project Discovery* is a large project and it required many resources. It would have been difficult for one university to complete the project on its own.

Our **future challenges** include the following:

1. There is a need to "institutionalize" the realization that the approach to accounting education at Notre Dame has changed drastically, and that the new approach, rather than the old approach, is the approach of the future. The new approach is

much more labor intensive and it treats teaching as a scholarly activity. While competition, accreditation standards, and other factors may encourage continuous improvement, there is a danger that *Project Discovery* will be viewed as a one-shot activity. As the department experiences leadership changes, as the faculty faces renewed pressure for research productivity, will the process of accounting education improvement continue?

2.   A related challenge is to find the resources for continuous updating and modification of the curriculum. Course materials have a much shorter shelf-life than traditional textbook materials. Finding the necessary time and resources is a challenge. One solution may be better communication, documentation, and sharing materials among "change" schools.

3.   In general, we need to learn how to implement change more efficiently. While it is clear that the faculty is spending more time on teaching, research expectations have not decreased. The need for balancing and integrating teaching and research activities remains a difficult challenge.

4.   Since *Project Discovery* is still in the process of being implemented at Notre Dame, one of our remaining challenges is to complete the assessment task.

Conclusion

We believe that *Project Discovery* has been a great success at Notre Dame. The first *Project Discovery* class graduated in May, 1996. The students are doing well in the job market and they seem pleased with the quality of their accounting education. Another indicator of success is that our Junior class of 240 accounting majors is near an all-time high. Further evaluation and assessment will continue as we complete the project.

But as always, the final test of success will be a market test. Will future Notre Dame accountancy graduates be among the best and brightest? Will Notre Dame continue to be recognized as a leader in accounting education? We see no slackening of effort as we continue to pursue our mission and we welcome the market's assessment of our results.

Appendix 1
CURRICULUM ASSESSMENT PROGRAM

GOAL		OBJECTIVE: Students will:	ASSESSMENT MEASURES	TIME FRAME	USE OF RESULTS
COGNITIVE	Knowledge and Comprehension	Have high verbal and math aptitudes	SAT scores; G.P.A.	Start of junior year	
		Be able to apply accounting concepts and principles in a variety of contexts	Portfolio Analysis[1]	Senior year	
			Alumni Surveys	Senior year and two years later	
			Recruiter Surveys	Every three years	
	Critical Thinking Skills	Use correct inference and deduction, recognize assumptions, interpret evidence, and evaluate arguments	Diagnostic Critical Thinking Skills Test	Sophomore and senior years	
	Develop Global Adaptability	Work effectively in teams with diverse individuals	Alumni Surveys	Senior year and two years later	
			Recruiter Surveys	Every three years	
BEHAVIORAL	Enhance Communication Skills	Speak and write effectively on accounting topics	Portfolio Analysis (writing)	Senior year	Compile holistic results for each class; review for trends; implement improvements as needed
			Standardized Measurement of Oral Presentations	Annual review of faculty evaluations of a sample of student presentations	
	Develop Technological Aptitude	Be able to effectively use computers to solve accounting problems	Alumni Surveys	Senior year and two years later	
			Recruiter Surveys	Every three years	
	Develop Ethical Awareness	Accept ambiguity in business decision making	Tolerance for Ambiguity Instrument	Start of junior year and end of senior year	
			Faculty Ratings of Students' Ethical Awareness, Analysis and Decision making in Live Simulations and Class Discussions	Senior year	
AFFECTIVE	Satisfaction with Learning Environment	Be satisfied with their accountancy program and suggest improvements based on changing needs in the profession	Alumni Surveys	Last semester; two and five years after graduation	

[1]Faculty judgments of students' use of accounting knowledge based on portfolio of major assignments.

Chapter 13
UNIVERSITY OF VIRGINIA
McIntire School of Commerce

Type, Size and Mission of Accounting Program

The accounting program at the University of Virginia is composed of a Master of Science in Accounting degree program and an undergraduate "concentration" (our term for "major") leading to a Bachelor of Science degree in Commerce. Our school has been at a "steady state" student body for several years — approximately 600 undergraduate students in their third and fourth years of study at the University and about 50 students in the graduate program in accounting. Of the total number of undergraduates, about 100 are in accounting, with the others distributed among Finance, MIS, Marketing, Management, and International Management. Students are admitted to our school following two years of study in the College of Arts & Sciences or at other universities. Roughly 70 percent of a new class comes from within the University. Average SAT scores are usually about 1200. There is no evening or part-time program and almost no adjunct faculty.

The Accounting Area mission statement, which follows below, guides the direction of the program.

The accounting area — consisting of faculty, curriculum and staff — is an integral component of the McIntire School of Commerce and the University of Virginia. It is dedicated to the professional practice of accounting and to advancing the art of organizational administration. Thus, the area recognizes four independent sets of responsibilities, namely, to the:

- Accounting Area
- McIntire School of Commerce
- University of Virginia
- Accounting profession and other sectors where accounting and financial management are practiced

As such, the accounting area is obliged to assist in carrying out the School's and the University's missions and in achieving their goals, and to contribute to the welfare and progress of external constituencies that rely on our efforts with respect to teaching, research and service. In addition, we are committed to continual improvement in our work and contributions and service to students, colleagues, the School, the University, and other constituencies.

Accounting concentrators complete a core business curriculum and a set of accounting courses. Prior to our AECC grant work, the accounting curriculum consisted of one year each of Introductory and Intermediate Accounting, and Commercial Law. One semester courses were also required in Cost Accounting & Cost Management, Auditing, Accounting Theory, and Taxation. As such, the curriculum was not significantly different from many others across the country.

Characteristics of the Program Before the Grant

The curriculum did not provide sufficient flexibility for some students while at the same time it allowed other students to focus too closely on accounting studies. Classes rarely required writing assignments. Virtually all classes were based on problem solving — both in lectures and homework assignments — dedicated to the learning and application of rules. Team projects were seldom employed. Classes were administered with rigor and high expectations of student performance and a highly motivated and disciplined student body responded accordingly. These students were, and continue to be, highly sought after by firms recruiting at the School.

Central Objectives of the Grant

We set forth certain objectives for ourselves and our curriculum. These were:

1. To attract a student to the accounting area of concentration who is interested in a broader-based education, and thus, will take advantage of the expanded number of electives that have been made available in our revised curriculum. To produce a more broadly educated individual.

2. To make professional accounting education a "five-year" curriculum.

3. To attract a student who is different in personality from those who now, and in past years, have elected to major in accounting. Past students have had a low tolerance for ambiguity and uncertainty and possessed a "right answer" mentality. They have also had a lower tolerance for other personality types and alternative points of view.

4. To promote a greater awareness of the need for creativity in problem-solving, and to develop this quality in our students. A concomitant feature of improved problem-solving skills is good judgment, a quality we hope to better develop in our students.

5. To cultivate in our students an appreciation of the need for "learning to learn."

6. To develop students' writing, presentation and interpersonal skills.

Key Means of Accomplishing Grant Objectives

A senior member of the accounting faculty began by drafting a model for discussion purposes that would serve as a springboard for the faculty's deliberations. The model was influenced by the Bedford Committee Report and the "Big Eight" white paper, as well as by the changes that were taking place in the profession, such as the 150-hour education requirement. With this draft paper, the accounting faculty held meetings in which changes and refinements were made and which led to a final proposal to the AECC. Our initial proposal was not accepted, thus leading to a second round of drafting and discussions — finally culminating in a proposal that was accepted.

During the grant period we also met with the Finance Area faculty — which had been most vocal in voicing their concerns — and spelled out in detail what changes would be made and how they would affect the School. We brought the project to the total School faculty and carefully explained what would happen and asked for their approval of the changes. These "open air" sessions with the faculty were very important in winning their concurrence and enabling our agenda to successfully move onward.

Major Changes from Pre-Grant Conditions and Circumstances

The AECC grant project did result in many major changes to our accounting program and the School. For example, a stepped up interest in **using information technology** occurred. The introductory financial accounting course, which had never employed computer assignments in the past because of the large enrollment, introduced computer homework assignments (Lotus-based and General Ledger package-based). Several courses are using multi-media and presentation packages as well as videos.

A second change of substance has been the introduction of what might be called **new educational activities and expectations for students.** Techniques such as "think-pair-share" are now commonly used, as well as student team projects and presentations. We expect students to learn a great deal on their own and in concert with their peers — for example, team homework is encouraged or required in many classes. A greater willingness to experiment and to question the conventional wisdom of accounting education has developed among the faculty. Faculty enthusiasm and pride in our new approaches remain high.

As a result of curriculum restructuring and our internal efforts to advise students on the merits of a fifth year of studies, we have witnessed a gradual **growth of interest in the M.S.** in Accounting program.

With the reduced number of classes required for concentration, we are seeing an unexpected increase in the number of students designing **new "double concentrations"** which involve coupling accounting with MIS, finance or other areas of study. We are also witnessing more accounting students completing a "minor" in the College of Arts and Sciences (e.g., languages).

Still another major change, described above, is the use of trained and carefully monitored **graduate students to deliver most introductory accounting courses.** Were it not for the emergence of a willingness to try something new, this bold experiment would not have been attempted. After the fall 1995 semester, applications to our School jumped 25% — an effect generally attributed to the excellent experience these students had in the Introductory Financial Accounting course.

The curriculum changes that were made at the undergraduate level caused **the accounting area to become more like the other areas** (Marketing, Finance, etc.), thus assuaging a source of minor irritation that had existed for years. In the past Accounting was perceived as being different, a fact that was explained and justified on the grounds that we had to do certain things to satisfy CPA exam requirements.

The last major change from pre-grant conditions and circumstances focuses on the CPA firms. By instituting the changes we and others have made in response to the call of the largest public accounting firms, we felt confident that the new curriculum would be enthusiastically received. Thus, we expected a very positive reaction that could have been manifested in numerous ways. Instead, we were met at the local level with no support and no recognition of the changes we had forged. The initiative started at the executive office level was literally being subverted by local office recruiters who advised our students that it wasn't necessary to stay in school for a fifth year. The major change came in **our attitude and anticipations.**

Once grant work began, we concentrated on making these changes, which are overlapping but, nonetheless, separate in thrust.

1. Modifying our pedagogical approach.

2. Restructuring the curriculum.

3. Revamping course content of our program.

Modifying Pedagogical Approach

The accounting faculty were in agreement on trying to teach in a different way; no one resisted. A main thrust of the grant project was to modify the pedagogy employed by our faculty and create new learning materials. We decided to:

1. Give up a "cover all the material attitude."

2. Place greater reliance on student self-learning.

3. Adopt the case approach as much as possible.

4. Expect students to develop judgment, communication skills, ability to deal with uncertainty, and, finally, to work toward broader based education.

Curriculum Restructuring

The major curriculum restructuring changes that were made as a result of the AECC grant work were:

1. Reducing undergraduate credit requirements in accounting. The undergraduate accounting concentration was reduced to nine credits and a limit established of three accounting elective courses.

2. Resequence some courses. For example, moved Commercial Law to second year; shifted Intermediate Accounting to one semester later in the third year to better integrate the subject matter with Corporate Finance.

3. Resequence the subject matter of the Cost Management class (which now became our "lead-off course" in the concentration) to better complement the subjects studied in Corporate Finance.

4. Several courses were transferred from the undergraduate to the graduate curriculum and renumbered: Advanced Accounting, Accounting Policy, Attestation, Auditing Seminar, and Not-for-Profit Accounting. These structural changes were designed to create a fifth year professional accounting program within which "technical content" courses would reside and to provide undergraduate students with a liberal accounting concentration. The latter would include only a few accounting courses and would limit the number of accounting courses that could be taken as electives so that students would have to take a fifth year of studies if they contemplated sitting for the CPA exam.

5. Prior to the last year of the grant project, we also designed two new courses for the graduate program which would complement the other changes we had undertaken. A three person team has been teaching "Global Competition" and a course in "Professional Practice Management," drawing upon partners from a number of accounting firms, has been offered. These were initial steps in a strategy designed to allow our program to better compete with MBA programs — the latter being a new focal point of recruiting for partner-caliber talent by CPA firms.

6. The accounting area coordinator was one of three faculty members making up a subcommittee which recommended to the faculty that all Commerce School students study a foreign language for two years. That recommendation had been included in the proposal that was originally submitted to the AECC. It was passed by the faculty and is a new requirement that strengthens our purpose of offering a broad-based liberal foundation of studies for accounting concentrators. A new core course, *International Business,* was also added as a School requirement at the same time.

7. An early admission policy was adopted allowing undergraduate students to secure early admission to the M.S. in Accounting program, thereby relieving much of the uncertainty that might otherwise have existed for them.

Revamping Course Content

The introductory courses (Financial and Managerial) began using group work and group testing, and refocusing the subject matter to put greater emphasis on management uses of information. The introductory financial accounting class, which was offered in a mass lecture format, proved to be an unsatisfactory medium for group work and testing, and that experiment was dropped. Work on a new textbook emphasizing a management approach to financial accounting continues. The second course (Managerial Accounting) has been successful and continues today. A new experiment in the Introductory Accounting class, however, has proved very successful. A two credit graduate course called "Teaching Practicum" was first developed during the summer of 1995 and then offered in the three weeks just before the start of the fall semester. The enrolled (11) graduate students had been hand picked and would ultimately teach small sections of the Introductory Accounting class. The class met five days a week, from nine a.m. to five p.m. to study teaching methods and philosophy. An extensive set of Power Point presentation slides were developed to guide the delivery of classes. All students followed a uniform syllabus and took identical examinations, which were designed by a senior member of the faculty who also taught two sections of the course.

The "Intermediate courses" focus on a large number of accounting issues which have been given a situational context through the use of a "master case" written by a member of our faculty and supporting multi-media software. The advanced cost-managerial courses are using case work which has been developed by the faculty. Similarly, Attestation (formerly Auditing) and Accounting Information Systems faculty have developed case materials and are integrating the two courses. Case development was also a significant aspect of the work done for the Accounting Policy course — a course which integrates subject matter from all of the subsets of accounting and relies heavily on group work.

Methods of Achieving Support

Initially we spoke with the Dean about the prospective project and grant proposal and gained his enthusiastic support. He assisted us in gaining the support of the Provost, who represented the central administration. A project director was selected. Our plans were laid out in terms of strategic objectives, a timetable, and budgetary requirements. During the grant period we also met with the Finance Area faculty — which had been most vocal in voicing their concerns — and spelled out in detail what changes would be made and how they would affect the School. We brought the project to the total faculty and carefully explained what would happen and asked for their approval of the changes. These "open air" sessions with the faculty were very important in winning their concurrence and enabling our agenda to successfully move onward. A central argument used in persuading all of the interested parties that our project was necessary was the 150-hour requirement that had already become law in many states.

Changes That Worked

We envisioned changes that could not be made and, therefore, were never attempted. We attempted other things that did not work and were abandoned. We tried many new things that worked reasonably well, but which had to be adjusted, and will keep on being adjusted in the future. Virtually nothing that we attempted turned out to be perfect the first time. Any faculty contemplating change should realize that they will have to continually make modifications and adjustments. Hoping to open up a box containing someone else's program to find a perfect model that only needs to be plugged into an electrical outlet like a new TV set is wishful thinking. Every school is in a different setting, dealing with slightly different circumstances — all of which should be taken into consideration when designing a new curriculum.

With those words of caution in mind, we think that what we have done overall is a decided improvement. There are schools — particularly urban institutions and schools with part-time programs — that will have extreme difficulty using group work. Some of the things we have developed will not work with large classes having enrollments of more than about 45 undergraduate students (e.g., case work, computer systems projects). The effect of shifting the accounting program emphasis from the undergraduate to the graduate level will have an effect on resource development. Most changes we and other schools have instituted have made a faculty member's work different and more intensive as they become the "guide on the side" instead of "the sage on the stage."

The changes we have made in the following courses should work elsewhere, with the noted qualifications:

Introductory Accounting must have computer resources and students must be able to work as teams on homework and projects.

Our Intermediate Accounting courses will work at other schools with a bright student body that is capable of doing substantial amounts of independent work and self-learning. Small classes are necessary (ours average 25 to 30 students).

Cost Management Accounting employs cases and computer assignments.

Attestation and Accounting Information Systems are highly coordinated and the subject matter is apportioned differently than in conventional course divisions. Students are required to do team assignments, including computer systems projects.

Several courses invite many speakers to address the students on specific subjects — particularly at the graduate level. Access to an available pool of skilled people is essential.

Software such as Lexus, Nexus and other data bases is employed in many classes.

Faculty will have to be available outside of class to a much greater extent than may have been true in the past for student guidance and counseling. Student grading and evaluation will take far more time than before in most cases.

Activities That Did Not Work

Group work in large classes is almost impossible to control and, consequently, many students become dissatisfied. The same thing is true of group tests. We abandoned group testing in our introductory accounting class. Recently, we abandoned mass lecture classes because we felt they were inconsistent with quality education.

We expected that success with our new program, which would bring with it increased enrollments at the graduate level, would be met with additional resources from the administration. Unfortunately, this proved to be wrong. Resources actually lessened and we found a bias against graduate education building in state government that continues to this day. As we move closer to the year 2000 and the exigencies of a 150 credit requirement become more immediate, pressures will build and may require us to make compromises.

Unexpected Benefits

We have enjoyed many benefits from the work we have done and the AECC grant. However, none were unexpected.

Measurement of the Effect of Changes Accomplished

Our curriculum restructuring was completed and is now reflected in the University Record and other school references.

An important objective we had was to promote and cultivate the skill of "learning to learn." At the start of the spring 1995 semester, students who had just completed the Intermediate Accounting sequence were given a test on a subject they had not studied before (concerning FAS Standard 115). They were given six hours to read the case and the Standard and write their answer. Their papers were graded and the resultant mean was 91 percent. The control group consisted of fourth year students who had completed the former, traditional intermediate accounting course the year before. The control group only scored a mean of 58 on a comparable test. Average SAT scores of both classes were approximately the same, suggesting that the innate ability of the two groups was not different. The faculty's personal observations support the test results indicating that the new pedagogy does develop a learning-to-learn skill.

Our ongoing assessment process involves:

1. Contemporaneous student feedback obtained from mid-semester questionnaires, daily feedback notes, and weekly meetings with quality control groups of students.

2. Student feedback questionnaires administered at the end of the semester to every student in every class.

3. A special assessment luncheon with a group of 10 to 12 graduate students, the area coordinator, and the School's Director of Graduate Studies where the students are given the opportunity to tell about their experiences and we can ask them questions in a confidential, non-threatening atmosphere.

4. A special luncheon with recruiters from major accounting firms and corporations to get their feedback on our graduates and the accounting curriculum.

5. One of our accounting classes has held a day at the end of the semester when student group presentations are made to a panel of judges from outside firms. These professional people give us another form of feedback on student performance, including public speaking ability.

We have no data as yet, on whether student personality types will change because the new curriculum attracts a different kind of student. Intuitively, we now think it will not — but that is no longer important. We believe that many skills can be taught to virtually any student and that the curriculum will deal with the propensity of those who gravitate to accounting to want one right answer.

Perpetuation Plans

Our new curriculum, pedagogy and enthusiasm for experimentation and questioning the conventional wisdom is so woven into the institutional fabric that we cannot imagine doing anything else. Is there a possibility that the program and faculty will slip back into its former mold? Absolutely not! No one here would tolerate it. We believe that a significant "shake out" of accounting programs across the country is coming and that the pioneers that add value in new ways will be the survivors. Schools that can't or won't change are going to be tomorrow's academic "buggy whips."

Dissemination

Over the past several years we have received many written requests for assistance from other schools. Almost every one of these was unique and different, being tantamount to a customized product. Another factor which makes replies difficult is that things are continuously being refined and improved, making it difficult to capture everything on paper. Thus, we suggest to those seeking assistance that they make a visit to our school and observe classes and discuss the issues in which they are interested with the instructors. To arrange a visit, contact our area coordinator.